SMALL STARTUP CITIES

How to Build a Thriving Startup Ecosystem in a Small City

Dominique Halaby

CITY CAMPUS PRESS

SAVANNAH

Originally published in paperback in 2026 by City Campus Press, Savannah, Georgia, USA

Ordering Information: Quantity sales. Special discounts are available on quantity purchases by corporations, associations, and others. For details, contact the email address above.

Designed by: *Muhammad Nouman*

The Library of Congress has cataloged the paperback edition as follows:
Halaby, Dominique
Small startup cities: how to build a thriving startup ecosystem in a small city / Dominique Halaby

p.   cm.

ISBN 979-8-9950606-0-4 (pbk)
ISBN 979-8-9950606-1-1 (epub)

1. Entrepreneurship. 2. New business enterprises. 3. Economic development. 4. Small cities—economic conditions. 5. Community development. I. Title

HD62.7 .S63 2026
338.040973—dc23   2026908326

To Maggie, Austin, Cameron, Isabella, Angelica and all those that dream of making their city a better place to call home.

And to Stephen Waldron whose editorial skills greatly contributed to the completion of this book.

CONTENTS

PART V: GROWING AND SUSTAINING MOMENTUM223

A Note from the Author

I didn't write this book because I believe small cities are behind. I wrote it because I know they're ready to build a community where entrepreneurs and innovators can thrive.

Over the past two decades, I've had the privilege of working with cities that rarely make national headlines but quietly carry the weight of America's economic future. Places where leaders wear multiple hats, where universities are deeply embedded in their communities, and where innovation isn't a buzzword; it's a necessity.

I've watched small cities reinvent themselves after the loss of an anchor employer. I've seen entrepreneurs launch companies not because it was trendy but because it was personal. I've worked alongside mayors, university presidents, economic developers, faculty, and founders who were tired of being told that innovation only happens somewhere else.

This book is for them.

It's for the city manager who knows their community has potential but needs a clearer roadmap.

It's for the university leader who wants to move beyond theory and into action.

It's for the economic developer who understands that recruiting alone won't secure the future.

And it's for the entrepreneur who chose to build in their community.

You won't find magic pills or silver bullets in these pages. What you will find are frameworks, lessons, and real-world examples drawn from places that decided to stop waiting for permission and start taking risks. This book highlights their stories: what works, what doesn't, and what I wish more communities understood before launching their first incubator, accelerator, or innovation initiative.

Most importantly, this book challenges a narrative that has gone unexamined for too long: that scale determines relevance. In my experience, proximity beats scale. Trust beats capital. And communities that align their assets, their people, institutions, and place can outperform far larger competitors.

You don't need to become the next Silicon Valley.

You don't need to chase every trend.

You don't need to outspend anyone.

But you do need clarity, commitment, and the courage to build something that fits your city.

Writing this book, just like building an ecosystem, was not a solo journey. I would like to thank the amazing people that I've had the privilege of working with all these years. These individuals are too numerous to list, but their stories and lessons learned are embedded in the pages of this book. I truly appreciate your commitment and dedication to growing your community.

For everyone else, I hope that this book will give you the confidence to start or the conviction to continue. That you find the resources and energy to show the world what we already know. Small cities don't need saving. They need believing in.

—Dominique Halaby

It was a really busy day. I was one of the finalists for a position in economic development at a Southern university located in a small rural community. After a series of interviews, I was asked to make a public presentation to a group of stakeholders in a newly renovated building that would serve as my unit's base of operations. At the time, the renovations weren't quite complete. The space that would later serve as offices was still barren. No walls. No doors. Only an open space, brimming with possibilities.

For my presentation, folding office chairs were brought in to give the space the illusion of a classroom. At the back of the space was an assortment of snacks and Southern-style sweet tea. Slowly, people began to trickle in. Then, as if they had been waiting around the corner, the rest arrived. All at once. Professors and prominent members of the community came to listen to my presentation but also to quiz me as to what I had in mind for the facility.

This gave me a chance to chat with a few community leaders before diving into my presentation. As I spoke about the importance of business research and gave examples of economic development projects that I led, I couldn't help but be caught up in what appeared to be an odd mix of enthusiasm and confusion. Toward the end of my presentation, I pivoted to asking them questions about their vision for the community.

There was a clear sense that the people in the room wanted to see the community grow. But there was an equal lack of alignment as to what that meant and how it would be achieved. They knew entrepreneurship was a key to helping residents capitalize on economic opportunities and to helping create new job opportunities for the city's youth. They felt so strongly in that purpose that the downtown development association had bought the foreclosed building that we were standing in and committed to renovating it to help build an entrepreneurship hub for the university. But they didn't really know how to do it.

They spoke of bringing entrepreneurship classes to the new facility. Of constructing offices to accommodate a business research unit. And of establishing a satellite of the university bookstore. While the plan was unclear, the passion for the community and the desire to build something with impact were.

Following the exchange of numerous platitudes and engaging chats, I went back to my hotel and called my wife.

Her first question was, "How did it go?"

I can still recall telling her, "I'm not sure."

"What do you mean?" she said.

"I'm not sure what to make of it. They want me to be in charge of this thing called the City Campus, but it's neither a city nor much of a campus."

Now keep in mind, I was born in New York City and grew up in Houston. To me, the name "City Campus" was more an oxymoron than a true identifier of the space. It was really only part of a small building in a town of 30,000.

I couldn't tell if the term "City Campus" was meant to be the actual name of the structure or whether it was only a placeholder until a more accurate one could be determined.

"But what about the community?" she asked. "Does it seem like a place that we could call home?"

The city itself was charming. While there were a lot of empty buildings downtown and little foot traffic to speak of, the possibilities were evident. And the "City Campus" was less than a mile from the main one.

And within an hour's drive, you had a major airport, a growing seaport, and access to one of the most historic cities in the South. The people were friendly. The traffic was nonexistent. And having the university as a community anchor exuded the sense of civic pride typically only found in a college town.

As I began to describe the community to her, I started to believe in its potential. I even started to see things in the facility and connect the dots between the stakeholders' desires for entrepreneurial growth and regional assets in a way that got me excited. The more we spoke, the more I became convinced that—"Yes. We could call this place home."

Before finally agreeing to relocate, we made two more visits to the community. We even brought our kids to see how they would react. Each time, I saw something new. A new opportunity that could be exploited but wasn't. A new chance to make a difference in my would-be home.

By the time I committed to relocate, I had already identified partners to engage with and funding opportunities to help build something special.

While I've been active in many communities, I primarily draw from my experience in Georgia for several reasons. First, there was my lack of familiarity with the area before I arrived. You don't need to be viewed as an insider to have an impact on your community. Your community is your home whether you've lived there your entire life or just arrived. You don't have to have generational ties to an area to institute change. You just have to have passion and a playbook.

Second, I want to dispel the belief that density is a prerequisite for entrepreneurial growth. While it no doubt helps, it isn't mandatory. Sure, it's much easier to identify 100 passionate and talented innovators in a city of 5 million than one with 5,000. But innovators and entrepreneurs are everywhere. You simply have to find the right reason and the right place for them to gather and connect. Trust me. They are there.

Third, I chose this experience to dispel the notion that change requires a top-down approach to leadership. In my first 10 years since we unpacked the boxes and began to call the community home, I went through three mayoral changes, four city managers, and five university presidents. While strong and consistent leadership at the community or institutional level is good, when it comes to building a startup ecosystem, that leadership can come from all areas of the community.

If you are passionate about making a difference in the area you call home, I'm here to tell you to look in the mirror. Start making the contacts and committing the energy to make it happen.

Finally, as our efforts grew from a single building to an award-winning entrepreneur support organization with six buildings spread across four different cities, I began to receive inquiries about how to replicate our success in other markets. Each time, people brought great energy to the conversation and believed that if we could achieve success, then why couldn't they? And they were right to think that. All they needed to know was how we did it.

But it wasn't just about growing an ecosystem. It was also about maintaining what we've built.

People change jobs. They relocate. And every time, a certain amount of institutional knowledge is lost. And when a new person comes in, there is a degree of re-education required. This change in personnel, especially early in the development of an ecosystem, leaves open the possibility that everything could fall apart. That means that a change in an ecosystem leader could mean that the effort to create something special would sometimes be starting from zero—if at all.

This means that every time someone new joins the ecosystem, a lot of energy and time is spent educating them, getting them to speak the same language, and making sure they are buying into a shared vision. In a mature ecosystem, there are plenty of places for someone new to fit in. To find their people. And to find their place.

But in a new ecosystem where things aren't yet defined, this can be distracting and stall momentum. It can be frustrating to the new person who doesn't feel that their ideas are being valued and to the people with historical knowledge who feel as though these new ideas have already been tried.

One thing I've learned is that it is great to have passionate people, but when one person's passion starts to infringe on another person's, conflict that may not be easily resolved can arise.

So I wrote this book as a way to tell not just our story and outline the steps to building a startup ecosystem but also to help you communicate what needs to happen and why.

Not everyone, not even the most visionary leader, is great at communicating that vision in a way that allows everyone to see themselves in it. This book is intended to help bridge that gap. It will help you craft your ecosystem story and communicate it in a way that aligns multiple stakeholders.

Ask any choir director, and they'll tell you that it's a lot easier to get everyone singing the same song if you give them the sheet music. Now, go out and gather your founders, funders, and supporters.

Treat this book as your city's sheet music. It's time to start harmonizing so you can go sing something special. Something that only your city can sing.

Introduction:
Small Doesn't Mean
Stagnant

---

*"I believe in America, as long as we're celebrating
the next generation of entrepreneurs, how we're
doing it everywhere, not just in a few places."*

- Steve Case, *Rise of the Rest*

When most people talk about startup ecosystems, their minds jump to the usual suspects—Silicon Valley, the Research Triangle, and Kendall Square. And why not? These ecosystems are located near major urban areas that play host to some of the best-endowed research institutions on the planet. Institutions where millions of dollars of cutting-edge research is conducted every day. They're near major cities that feature companies with billion-dollar valuations, consistently launch unicorn startups, and have a steady stream of demo days, pitch competitions, and venture capital firms competing for the next big exit. At the end of the day, these are the ecosystems that dominate headlines and shape our views on what innovation and entrepreneurship ought to look like.

But what about the rest of the country? What about the cities with populations under 200,000 and without globally recognized universities? What about the towns struggling to create communities where ideas can flourish, innovative businesses can launch, and creative individuals want to call home? The places where you are just as likely to encounter the mayor at the grocery store as you are at an official ribbon-cutting event. The places where, on certain weekends, downtowns not only turn into farmers' markets but also into gathering places where neighbors unite and support local businesses. The places where congestion means coping with the occasional tractor on a two-lane road. These are the places where community means more than just a place you hang your hat; it's where you hang your heart.

These are the cities that have too often been left out of the innovation narrative. Not because they lack talent or ideas, but because they've been implicitly (and sometimes explicitly) told that real innovation only happens in areas with soaring rents and sprawling tech campuses. And that if you're not in one of these tech hubs, you're behind.

But that's a myth. And it's one we need to dismantle.

This book is for the cities between the coasts. For the communities that still believe in the power of reinvention. For the local leaders, educators, entrepreneurs, and risk-takers who see promise in old buildings, potential in underutilized assets, and talent in people who never saw themselves as startup founders.

It's for the places where startup ecosystems don't just need to be built—they can be built. Not in spite of being small, but because of it. The very fact that these cities are smaller, less resourced, and hungrier is the very reason they are primed for innovation.

Think for a moment. If I gave you unlimited resources and dropped you off halfway around the world and told you to return in a week, how much innovation would you use? Once you determined where you were, you would simply buy a ride to the nearest airport and purchase an airline ticket. You would probably take in a few sights along the way and spend money on things you didn't need to accomplish the task.

But imagine if I gave you only $100. You would barter and hustle. You would convince others to help you on your journey and tap into every resource you could imagine to accomplish your task. That hunger, that spirit—that's the driver of true innovation. That is what small communities need to tap into. Stop worrying about the lack of resources and start identifying where you are. Tap into your resources, sell your story, and convince others to join you on your journey.

The Narrative is Changing

For far too long, the story of innovation has been told through a narrow, coastal lens. It's a narrative that suggested if you wanted to be part of the startup world and to really be taken seriously, you had to leave your hometown behind. You had to chase opportunity to the Bay Area, to Boston, to Brooklyn. You had to uproot your life, conform to a culture you didn't create, and play by rules you didn't write.

From Statesboro, Georgia, to St. George, Utah, and from Greenville, South Carolina, to Green Bay, Wisconsin, small and mid-sized cities across America are rediscovering what they've always had: resilience, resourcefulness, and a deep-rooted sense of community. These are places with histories of entrepreneurship. Places where small businesses once lined every main street and local ingenuity powered local economies. They may not have been called "startups" back then, but make no mistake, the spirit was the same.

Today, these cities are reclaiming that legacy. They're leaning into what makes them unique rather than trying to imitate Silicon Valley. They're showing that proximity breeds trust, that authenticity can outperform polish, and that real community—the kind built on shared values and generational ties—is not a limitation. It's a competitive advantage.

And perhaps most importantly, these communities are proving that you don't need a unicorn to build an ecosystem. You don't need billion-dollar valuations to validate your efforts or attract outside attention. You just need passionate, committed people. You need a shared vision that aligns institutions, investors, and innovators. And you need patience. The kind of patience that manifests a long-term commitment that refuses to be derailed by quarterly metrics or the lack of headlines.

This new wave of startup cities isn't waiting for permission. They're building on their own terms. And they're rewriting the playbook as they go.

Why I Wrote This Book

I've spent the better part of my career working at the crossroads of economic development, higher education, and innovation, especially in the kinds of communities that rarely make the cover of business magazines. These are cities that may not have Fortune 500 headquarters or sprawling innovation districts, but they have something far more important: grit, ingenuity, and people who care deeply about the places they call home.

Typically, I would plug in to the community, help identify gaps in the ecosystem, and work to build a coalition to help channel the local energy to something greater than the individual parts. Something more. Something special.

Each time I did that in one community, I would get questions from others. And I kept hearing the same set of questions:

- "How do we get something started here?"

- "What does a real startup ecosystem even look like in a city like ours?"

- "Can we really do this without outside capital or a flashy tech sector?"

And the answer to all of those questions is a resounding yes.

Yes, you can start something where you are.

Yes, you can build a startup ecosystem that supports local founders and fosters innovation.

And yes, you can do it without waiting on permission from a renowned investor or a national foundation.

The thing to keep in mind is that you can't just copy and paste what worked in Palo Alto or Boston and expect it to thrive in your community. While your efforts to build an ecosystem may be new, your city isn't a blank canvas. It's a living, breathing place that has its own history, culture, values, and challenges. That's not a problem to work around. That's the foundation to build on.

True startup ecosystems are not imported; they're grown. They take root in what already exists. This ecosystem is built by people who believe in possibilities, institutions willing to collaborate, local stories that shape identity, and a collective willingness to engage in the hard, slow, often unglamorous work of building trust and momentum.

This book is a blueprint for that kind of work. It's not a "one-size-fits-all" model. It's a guide to help communities discover their own way forward. A way that's authentic, sustainable, and deeply aligned with who they are and who they aspire to become.

What You'll Learn

This isn't a theoretical text or a high-level policy brief. It's a hands-on, practical guide written for the people who are doing the work—or who want to. It's for economic developers trying to spark momentum in overlooked regions. It's for educators who are shaping the next generation of innovators. It's for civic leaders navigating public–private partnerships. It's for nonprofit professionals bridging gaps and building trust. For founders and funders. And yes, it's for everyday residents who may not hold an official title but care deeply about seeing their hometown thrive.

Because building a startup ecosystem isn't about waiting for the right consultant or capital infusion to arrive. It's about getting started—thoughtfully, strategically, and with a clear sense of purpose.

In the pages ahead, we'll break it down step-by-step. We'll talk about:

- What a startup ecosystem actually is and, just as importantly, what it's not.

- How to identify the right stakeholders and bring them to the table, even when they've never worked together before.

- What infrastructure and resources truly matter, so you can focus your energy where it counts.

- How to support founders in meaningful ways that go beyond pitch nights and one-off events.

- What it takes to attract funding, tell your city's story with authenticity, and build something that lasts.

- Why inclusion isn't just a buzzword or something to ignore. It's a foundational strategy. Because if the same few voices always lead the charge, you'll keep getting the same limited results.

- And what to measure and, just as critically, what to ignore.

Each chapter is designed to be actionable. You'll find real-world examples from communities that look more like yours than like San Jose or Seattle. You'll get checklists you can use right away, along with insights and lessons pulled from lived experience—not just theory.

This book isn't about admiring the idea of innovation. It's about building it, block by block, in the places that need it most.

Things to Remember

First, it's important to clarify that in this book, the term *startup* encompasses more than just technology. It doesn't mean apps, algorithms, or billion-dollar valuations. It doesn't require a hoodie, a pitch deck, or a venture capitalist on speed dial.

A startup, as we define it here, is any new venture that solves a problem, creates value, and has the potential to grow—period. That might be a mobile food truck serving underserved neighborhoods. It could also be a digital marketplace that connects local farmers to a national audience. Or a community health solution developed by a health professional who sees gaps in the system that no one else is addressing.

Broadly speaking, innovation isn't limited to new cutting-edge products or technology. It lives wherever people see a need and work to meet it with creativity, courage, and action.

And being an entrepreneur isn't just limited to young people. Yes, there are 22-year-old founders building ambitious ideas from dorm rooms and coffee shops, but there are also side-hustling parents launching ventures between school drop-offs. There are immigrants leveraging their global experience to build businesses rooted in local opportunity. There are veterans who've led teams in complex environments and are now applying that same discipline to solve civilian problems. There are retirees who've spent decades mastering their craft and are finally launching the business they never had time to pursue.

Age, background, education level: none of these are barriers in a truly inclusive startup ecosystem. If you're building something new that matters, whether it's high-growth, high-tech, or high-impact, you're part of the story. And your city's ecosystem should recognize, support, and celebrate that.

That's the kind of entrepreneurship this book is about. Broad. Bold. Grounded in reality. And open to everyone willing to take that first courageous step.

You Don't Have to Wait

You don't need a seven-figure grant to get started. You don't need a gleaming, state-of-the-art incubator with designer furniture and a rooftop event space. And you certainly don't need a celebrity founder to give your city permission to dream big. What you do need is something much more powerful and far more attainable.

One of my all-time favorite quotes is attributed to the renowned anthropologist Margaret Mead: "Never doubt that a small group of thoughtful, committed individuals can change the world. In fact, it's the only thing that ever has." All you need to get your ecosystem off the ground is a small group of people who believe. People who see not just what their community is today, but what it could become. People who are willing to roll up their sleeves, take risks, and invest in a vision that might not yet exist on paper but lives vividly in their minds and hearts.

People who believe:

- That their city has the right AND the responsibility to create its own future, on its own terms.

- That talent is everywhere, even if opportunity isn't yet. And that with the right support, everyday people can do extraordinary things.

- That entrepreneurship isn't just about scaling fast or making headlines: it's a tool for equity, for ownership, for lifting people up and building wealth that stays rooted in the community.

- And that a startup ecosystem should reflect the heart, soul, and character of the place it serves. Not try to imitate a city it will never be.

If you see yourself in that vision. If you've ever looked around your community and thought, "We can do more. We can do better. And we don't have to wait for someone else to do it for us," then you're exactly where you need to be.

This book was written for you.

Let's get to work. Let's build.

PART I

UNDERSTANDING THE LANDSCAPE

CHAPTER 1:
WHAT IS A STARTUP ECOSYSTEM?

"Though no one can go back and make a brand new start, anyone can start from now and make a brand new ending."

- Carl Bard, *Pulitzer-Prize-Winning Author*

When looking at successful ecosystems, it's easy to look at their assets and think, "If only we had a major university…" Or "If only we had venture capital money…" The issue with the "if only we had this or that" argument is that it focuses too much on what you lack rather than on what you have.

Remember that an ecosystem is a complex system of living organisms. And different organisms (or entities) need different conditions to thrive. You would never try to transplant the majestic redwoods of California to the beaches of South Florida and expect them to be successful, would you? Similarly, you wouldn't consider relocating sequoia cacti from Arizona to

Alaska and expect them to thrive? Of course not. Those regions simply don't have the right environment for them to grow and flourish.

So, build your own ecosystem. Build around your community assets. Stop trying to build "something like Austin" or "something like Boulder," and start understanding and appreciating the assets in your ecosystem.

Whether it's proximity to a major port, access to an international market, or accessible leadership and policymakers, every city has something special to offer. Especially yours.

A Startup Ecosystem Defined

A startup ecosystem is a network of people, organizations, values, and infrastructure that work together to help entrepreneurs from the moment they come up with an idea until they grow, pivot, or start over. It includes colleges, banks, city officials, accelerators, libraries, mentors, local media, and, most importantly: the entrepreneurs themselves.

And just like any other living thing, its health depends on how well its pieces work together. The ecosystem suffers when communication breaks down or when one part takes over at the expense of the others. Only when the elements work together, trust each other, and share ownership does genuine growth occur.

This chapter sets the stage for that kind of real and exciting progress. The kind of growth that will make the news and impact your community's very fabric. Before we can develop anything useful, though, we need to agree on what we want and how to talk about it. We need to know what we're doing, its significance, and how we'll work together to do it.

First, let's have a clear picture of what a startup environment is and what it implies for your area.

An Ecosystem Is Not a Program

When thinking about what a startup ecosystem is, you also have to consider what it isn't. For starters, a startup ecosystem is not a single program, event, or building.

You can have the most beautifully designed incubator in the heart of your downtown with modern architecture, exposed brick, open workspaces, and all the right buzzwords on the walls and still have no functioning startup ecosystem. You can host a pitch competition every year, bring in keynote speakers, hand out oversized checks, and still see little to no sustained entrepreneurial growth.

Why? Because ecosystems aren't built from isolated moments or flashy initiatives. They're built on interconnectedness. On relationships. On trust, infrastructure, culture, and consistency. A successful startup ecosystem is less about a single program, center, or initiative and more about how effectively and seamlessly they work together.

In actuality, your startup ecosystem is like a garden. You don't grow a thriving garden just by planting a few seeds and hoping for the best. You need the right conditions, the right environment, and the right people tending it every single day. You need to water it, nurture it, and remove the weeds.

First, you need fertile soil. That's your culture. A culture that embraces risk, celebrates local entrepreneurs, and sees failure not as a dead end but as a stepping stone.

You need water. That's capital. Not just venture dollars, but local banks, community lenders, friends and family networks, and flexible, early-stage funding.

You need sunlight. That's support. Mentorship, technical assistance, storytelling, networks, everything that helps founders, also known as entrepreneurs, grow stronger and more confident.

You need space to grow. I don't necessarily mean a physical space like an incubator. I mean policy. Zoning, permitting, procurement practices, and local regulations that either nurture innovation or stifle it.

And finally, you need a gardener. That's leadership. Someone (or ideally, a coalition of people) who sees the big picture, connects the dots, and keeps the vision moving forward through all the seasons of growth and challenge.

If even one of these elements is missing—or worse, misaligned—then your garden struggles. The seeds may be there. The intention may be there. But nothing flourishes.

This chapter is about making sure the ground you're building on is ready, not just for planting, but for long-term growth because ecosystems aren't born from ribbon cuttings or press releases. They're cultivated with care, intention, and a whole lot of collaboration.

The Components of a Startup Ecosystem

While ecosystems vary from one community to the next and depend on things like their geography, industry mix, demographics, and history, almost all healthy, functioning ecosystems share a set of common core elements. And while all the components are important to creating a vibrant ecosystem, it's important to stay founder-focused and place the entrepreneurs at the center.

1. Entrepreneurs (The Core)

Let's not overcomplicate this—*people,* not programs, build startups.

Not buildings. Not brands. *People.*

The founders are at the heart of any thriving startup ecosystem. The doers. The risk-takers. The ones who stay up late refining their prototype, who max out their savings to pursue an idea, who get back up after the third "no," and who, against all odds, decide to build something where nothing existed before.

Admittedly, keeping your ecosystem focused on the founder isn't easy. This is especially true since you're trying to get things to take root and balance competing priorities. Elected officials want to see headlines. Supporters want to feel good about their contributions. And investors want to see a return. Everyone has a different motivation for what they want, but the entrepreneur is the heartbeat of the ecosystem. Everything else, every coworking space, every funding program, every pitch night, every accelerator, is secondary. Those things should *exist to support the founder,* not to serve as the focal point.

If your ecosystem is doing great events, but founders still feel isolated, or if your city is making splashy announcements but can't point to five local entrepreneurs who feel genuinely supported, then something's off.

A founder-first ecosystem listens to its entrepreneurs. It asks:

- What do they need?

- Where are the friction points in their journey?

- Are they spending more time navigating bureaucracy than building their business?

- Do they feel *seen, heard, and valued?*

If you aren't intentionally operating with a founder-first mindset, you risk developing a community that is the antithesis of what you are trying to build. Rather than creating a city that attracts and retains entrepreneurs, your city may end up becoming one that quietly drives them away.

If your founders feel isolated, burned out, or invisible, it doesn't matter how many programs you have. If the entrepreneur isn't thriving, neither is the ecosystem.

2. Support Organizations (The Infrastructure)

Once you've centered the entrepreneur, the next question should be "Who's helping them along the way?"

That's where support organizations come in. These are the players who make the path a little smoother and the climb a little less steep. Think university-based innovation centers, incubators, accelerators, small business development centers (SBDCs), makerspaces, coworking hubs, economic development offices, chambers of commerce, and nonprofit initiatives focused on entrepreneurship.

This isn't just about making it easier on the entrepreneur; it's about positively impacting the trajectory of their business. Every time an entrepreneur successfully engages with a support organization, it creates a new inflection point and positively alters that business's trajectory for success.

Let's face it: Some entrepreneurs will be successful regardless of who they engage with. You know the type. Their sheer will is like a force of nature. They appear to have the "it" factor. The right idea. The right timing. The right strategy.

But the truth is, they also know when to seek help along the way and when to tap into their network. Even "self-made" billionaire entrepreneurs like Mark Zuckerberg, Jeff Bezos, Elon Musk, and Michael Dell received financial and emotional support from their parents early in their entrepreneurial journey.

Whether from established support organizations, key mentors, or family and friends, launching a new venture takes support. This support is crucial to reducing friction and moving the business along as smoothly and quickly as possible.

When done right, supporters (and support organizations) help founders navigate early-stage challenges faster and smarter. They help clarify the messy middle between "I have an idea" and "I have traction." They offer access to mentorship, business modeling, prototyping, market validation, and occasionally, capital readiness. In short, they make the invisible visible and the impossible more manageable.

Support organizations have a critical role to play, but their impact is multiplied when they work as part of a larger, intentional network. For example, imagine that an entrepreneur takes an idea to a meeting with a colleague at a local coffee shop. The colleague refers the entrepreneur to an entrepreneurship center at the local university to help with customer discovery. From there, the entrepreneur begins creating a prototype at the local makerspace. The lab manager connects the entrepreneur with a business research unit to get help identifying the target market. The unit is in the same area as a coworking space that the entrepreneur joins to build credibility and to find their people. Another member of the coworking space tells the entrepreneur about an upcoming pitch competition at a local accelerator, and the entrepreneur decides to compete. The director of the local SBDC is in the audience and offers to review the entrepreneur's business plan and discuss securing an initial loan. Members of a local angel investment group, interested in funding the venture, are also in the audience and impressed with the pitch.

The Power of Entrepreneurial Support Organizations

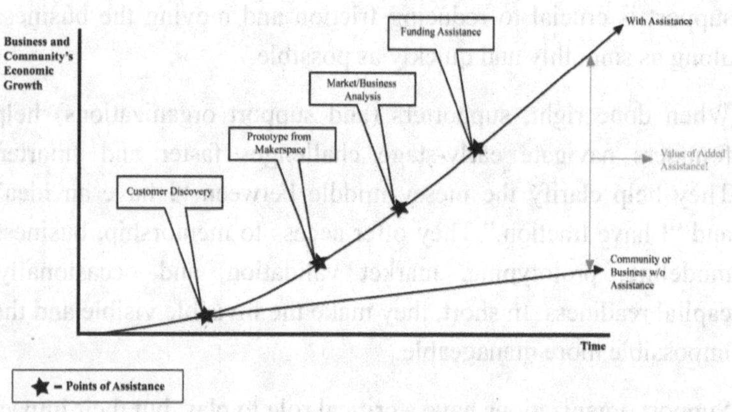

When done right, the entrepreneur is able to travel smoothly through the ecosystem. No repetition. Just forward momentum.

But this type of operational efficiency doesn't just happen. It requires coordination and trust among and between the support organizations. It requires that these organizations break down silos and adopt a founder-first philosophy that may require the organization to subjugate their individual processes to the broader ecosystem.

If there is no coordination of services. No communication between organizations. No shared metrics. No referrals. No coordination. It's not an ecosystem; It's chaos disguised as progress.

Why is this important? Because if three organizations are offering overlapping pitch prep sessions and no one knows who's attending what, or if a founder has to tell their story from scratch at every stop, you're not building community. You're creating confusion. You're wasting time. And you're exhausting the very people you claim to support.

The goal shouldn't be to do more. The goal should be to do it better. You should focus on coordinating activities and not duplicating them because when these groups share knowledge, pool resources, and center the entrepreneur above all else, the entire system becomes stronger.

In a healthy ecosystem, support is seamless, not siloed.

3. Access to Capital (The Fuel)

The fastest production car in the world is now the SSC Tuatara. With a top speed of 331 mph, this American-made car with a 5.9-liter engine and twin-turbo V8 can accelerate from zero to 60 in 1.6 seconds! But how fast do you think it goes on an empty tank of gas?

Just like the SSC Tuatara, no matter how passionate a founder is, no matter how groundbreaking the idea, they won't get far without fuel. And in the world of startups, that fuel is capital.

Unfortunately, for smaller cities and underrepresented communities, early-stage funding is almost always the weakest and most fragile part of the ecosystem.

It's easy to say, "We need venture capital." It's harder to admit that most VC firms aren't coming to your town anytime soon, at least not until they see a track record, a pipeline, and a reason to believe there's value on the ground.

So you can't wait for Marc Andreessen and a16z to take notice and come knocking. You need to build your own runway. And that means getting creative, very creative, about how you help founders access the resources they need to take the first few steps.

This might take one of many forms. For starters, your city, university, or local foundation could offer microgrants to help entrepreneurs remove early friction and validate ideas. Angel groups, even if they start informally, can go a long way in helping entrepreneurs get initial traction. A few successful business owners pooling capital, regardless of whether they meet the SEC standard to be investors, can be a great start.

Entrepreneurs can use a variety of methods to raise capital. Providing education that teaches entrepreneurs about crowdfunding and how to tap their own networks for funds, as well as how to tell their story in a way that resonates, can be extremely valuable.

You can even work with corporate sponsors to fund idea-stage projects. This is particularly beneficial if your ecosystem has a makerspace and if there's a natural alignment between startup activity and industry needs.

This isn't just about raising more money. It's about lowering the cost of starting.

When founders don't need $250,000 to test a concept, when they can prototype, iterate, and launch in smaller, smarter steps, you start to unlock the kind of inclusive entrepreneurship that doesn't rely on privilege, pedigree, or proximity to capital hubs. They're on their way to

creating a financial culture that says, "If you've got a good idea and the drive to pursue it, we'll find a way to help you get started."

That's what healthy ecosystems do.

4. Talent & Education (The Pipeline)

Startups don't scale on vision alone. Every founder eventually faces the same challenge: building a team that can help turn an idea into something real and sustainable.

Which means every startup ecosystem needs a reliable talent pipeline.

However, when it comes to talent development in entrepreneurship, there's good news and bad news. The good news is that most small and mid-sized cities in America already have the ingredients: local colleges, community colleges; technical schools; even high schools with strong career and technical education (CTE) programs. These institutions are talent factories where the next generation of creators, builders, and problem-solvers are already being trained.

The bad news: unless entrepreneurship is embedded in the educational experience, these institutions end up preparing students to fill jobs, not to create them.

That's a missed opportunity. A big one.

If we want to build startup ecosystems that last, we need to stop treating education and entrepreneurship as separate paths. They should be part of the same strategy. Take for example, Stanford University and MIT, institutions widely regarded for fostering a culture of innovation and entrepreneurship. These schools play a key part in the development and growth of their startup ecosystems. That's in large part because at these institutions concepts like innovation and entrepreneurship are less about a specific program and more about how people think regardless of what degree program or discipline they find themselves in. These schools are really good at attracting individuals with an entrepreneurial mindset and fostering it in newcomers.

For you, that means working with area colleges and universities to encourage entrepreneurship minors or certificate programs, so students from any major can learn the basics of launching a venture. That means creating opportunities for students to intern at local startups, not just big corporations, so that they can experience the scrappiness, urgency, and innovation that define early-stage companies.

It means hosting startup boot camps and hackathons on campus and giving students a safe space to test ideas, meet collaborators, and build confidence. It means supporting high school pitch competitions that show students entrepreneurship is not just for adults or techies. It's also for them.

This is important because if your startup ecosystem isn't engaging young people, it's not an ecosystem; it's a short-term project with a short-term future.

The most resilient entrepreneurial communities invest in talent early and often. They make it clear that innovation doesn't start after graduation; it starts now. In the classroom. In after-school clubs. In the side projects and basement ideas no one's taken seriously yet.

The next generation of founders is already here. The only question is whether we're giving them a reason and a roadmap to build right where they are.

5. Culture & Community (The Soul of the Ecosystem)

Famed management guru Peter Drucker famously said, "Culture eats strategy for breakfast." Perhaps nowhere is this more evident than in your startup ecosystem. Ecosystem culture is the piece everyone feels, but few can describe. It's elusive, hard to measure, and often goes overlooked in strategic plans and funding proposals. But your culture is the heartbeat of your ecosystem. It's the difference between a group of disconnected players and a true community moving in the same direction.

You can have a wide assortment of programs, funding, and talent, but without the right culture, nothing will stick. Culture is what fills in the gaps between the formal structures; it's what shows up when the cameras are off and the events are over.

Culture is how a city talks about risk—not just publicly, but in quiet conversations between colleagues and neighbors. It's how it treats the entrepreneur whose first business didn't work out. Is that person dismissed and forgotten? Or do they get a second look, a pat on the back, and a "What's next?"

It's whether two founders meet for coffee and share insights or avoid each other out of fear and scarcity.

It's whether mentors keep their networks close to their vest or open doors freely.

It's the vibe of your coworking spaces, the coverage from local media, and the tone of your pitch events.

It's who gets celebrated, who gets funded, and who gets ignored.

Perhaps the most important manifestation of culture can be felt in how your city tells its startup story. Is it a story about the few elite people who "made it?" Or is yours a story about grit and determination, taking risks, trying new things, and making progress—together?

Now, if you think having a startup culture is something that happens by accident, you're wrong. It has to be nurtured, patiently and intentionally. People need to hear your story, the full story, not just the highlight reel. Share the setbacks, the scrappy pivots, and the hard-earned lessons.

You need to be celebrating first steps, not just finish lines. That founder with five customers? They deserve recognition too. And start creating startup rituals in the community, like demo days, peer mentorship circles, founder dinners, or open mic nights. These help evangelize entrepreneurship and get people excited about the possibilities.

It's important to keep in mind that a thriving culture is one where founders don't feel like they're going it alone. They feel supported, not just by the organizations whose purpose is to help them succeed, but by the entire community. They know their scrappy startup is fighting the odds, but they believe their community roots for the underdog. Ever heard the saying "Keep Austin Weird?" Chances are that you have. It's often used to describe the laid-back, quirky style of the city that embodies a vibrant culture with an individual spirit. Austinite Red Wassenich coined that catchy slogan, which several other cities are now adopting, to support local businesses and artists by encouraging people to buy local. In Austin, what Red did so eloquently was galvanize local enthusiasm for small businesses—not just from the VC community, the support organizations, or the entrepreneurs themselves—but from the entire community. When entrepreneurs feel supported at that level, they feel safe enough to try and safe enough to fail.

If your local entrepreneurs feel isolated, invisible, or like outsiders in their own town, that's not a minor issue. It's a flashing red warning light because all the resources in the world can't compensate for a culture that stifles connection and confidence.

Conversely, when the culture is right and entrepreneurs know they're seen, supported, and part of something greater than themselves, ecosystems start to grow, not just in numbers, but in depth, durability, and heart.

And that's when your city stops chasing someone else's model and starts building its own.

6. Policy and Infrastructure (The Supporting Structure)

Your ecosystem is still a part of a larger system of rules, resources, and realities, no matter how passionate your founders are or how vibrant your culture grows. That's where policy and infrastructure come in.

Decisions made at the city council table, the priorities written into economic development plans, and the basic infrastructure (or lack thereof) that either empowers or frustrates entrepreneurs continuously shape ecosystems.

I want you to ask yourself the following:

- Can someone open a pop-up shop in your downtown without navigating a maze of outdated zoning laws?

- Can a food entrepreneur test a new concept without paying thousands in permitting or facility upgrades?

- Do local startups have access to reliable, affordable broadband—especially in rural or underserved areas?

- Are there public-sector dollars, like grants, matching funds, or procurement contracts from anchor institutions, accessible to early-stage ventures?

These aren't abstract issues. They're day-one obstacles that either open the door for new businesses or quietly close it before they start.

That's why local government matters so much. Cities that thrive don't just support entrepreneurs with words; they do it with policy. They stop thinking like regulators and start thinking like enablers.

They start by asking, "What would it look like if our policies made it easier, faster, and cheaper to start something new?"

Smart cities take actions that make their communities easy places to start something new. They take actions like streamlining the permitting process for small businesses and mobile vendors. They create innovation zones or startup districts that have flexible use policies. They offer reduced-cost leases in city-owned buildings and prioritize minority- and women-owned startups in procurement decisions. They even invest in infrastructure like coworking spaces, public Wi-Fi, or multi-use event facilities.

When your city takes action and adopts policies that make starting a business easy, it builds trust. It signals to the community that their leaders aren't just focused on chasing outside investment; they're invested in growing local talent, local ventures, and local ownership.

Ultimately, infrastructure isn't just roads and fiber lines; it's the scaffolding that holds up everything else: your people, your programs, and your momentum.

If you want a resilient, inclusive startup ecosystem, you have to create an environment where entrepreneurs aren't fighting the system just to exist. You have to bake entrepreneurship into your city's DNA.

In the strongest ecosystems, policy isn't an obstacle; It's a lever.

And local leaders aren't just administrators; they're architects of possibility.

The Ecosystem Flywheel (How Momentum Builds)

Whether you're in a big city, a small town, or somewhere in between, it's important to keep in mind that ecosystems don't explode into existence. They turn. Slowly. Deliberately. Then all at once.

That turning motion? That's what Jim Collins referred to as "the flywheel effect" in his book *Good to Great*.

In mechanical terms, a flywheel stores rotational energy. It's hard to get moving at first, but once it's spinning, it keeps spinning with less effort and greater force. In a startup ecosystem, that same principle applies.

Ecosystems are built through interlocking actions, with each one strengthening and accelerating the others over time. First, entrepreneurs take a leap, testing new ideas and creating energy at the center. Then, support organizations step in to reduce friction, helping those ideas take shape. Then funders, whether friends, family, local angels, grant makers, or city leaders, begin to invest time and capital with the belief that the concept has merit and that the entrepreneur has what it takes to deliver.

It is from there that success stories emerge. That 19-year-old college freshman who started selling computer parts in his dorm room in two years is occupying an 83,000-square-foot building on the north end of town. Suddenly, people are telling the story, and others are beginning to think, "If they can do it here, maybe I can too."

The culture shifts. Risk feels a little less risky. Collaboration feels more natural.

And more people join the movement. More founders, more mentors, more educators, and more civic leaders, each one adding momentum to the wheel.

At first, that flywheel can feel painfully slow. You host an event and only 10 people show up. A startup launches, then stalls. You try to coordinate organizations, but people are too busy or not sure how they fit in.

All I can tell you is to keep pushing.

Because what starts as a grind becomes a rhythm.

What felt like separate parts begins to function like a system.

And over time, the ecosystem builds a kind of self-sustaining motion.

Founders start to mentor newer founders.

One small success inspires five more attempts.

Funders who were once cautious become champions.

Civic pride swells, and the local media start paying attention.

New partnerships emerge, not because someone forced them, but because they just make sense.

That's the power of the flywheel. Once it's turning, it fuels itself.

But it's not magic. It's the product of intentional action, persistent belief, and cross-sector collaboration. Every spoke of the wheel (i.e., entrepreneurship, support, capital, education, culture, and infrastructure) has to connect and contribute.

If one part stops moving, the wheel slows.

But when they're all aligned? When the ecosystem starts generating its own momentum.

That's when ecosystems don't just exist; they accelerate.

And that's when a city starts to realize that we're not waiting for innovation to happen to us; we're building it ourselves.

Common Pitfalls to Avoid (Lessons From the Trenches)

Every city that sets out to build a startup ecosystem starts with energy, hope, and ambition. And that's a beautiful thing. But as with any complex system, even the best intentions can lead to unintended consequences.

Over the years, I've seen the same mistakes show up in communities of all sizes. They don't come from a lack of care; they usually come from misunderstanding what a true ecosystem is supposed to do.

So let's talk about a few of the most common traps—and how to avoid them:

1. Focusing on Events Over Outcomes

When I first started ecosystem building, I used to marvel at other startup ecosystems. They seemed to always have something on the calendar: an entrepreneur meetup, a pitch night, a training session on the lean model canvas. I thought these communities were the best and tried hard to copy their event schedules. But as time went on, I learned that a busy calendar doesn't guarantee that an ecosystem is healthy.

You can have weekly pitch nights, monthly mixers, and quarterly workshops, but if those events aren't helping founders start new businesses, work together more, or get real support, then you're just making noise.

Events are not answers; they are tools. They should exist in service to outcomes such as:

- Startups launched;

- Capital deployed;

- Partnerships formed;

- Founders supported;

- Talent retained.

Ask yourself after every initiative: Did this move the needle? Or did we just check a box?

At the end of the day, entrepreneurship isn't about optics; it's about outcomes.

2. Centralizing Authority

I also learned that ecosystems don't operate well when they are run from the top down. They are organic, spread out, and adaptive. So, no one organization, funder, or leader should strive to "own" everything. This is a particularly hard concept to grasp and truly appreciate, especially in a small city where you are more likely to feel a call to action. You are more likely to believe that if you don't do it, then who will? That feeling of being called to something. That burden of responsibility. I'm here to tell you that it's a good thing. It's probably why you're reading this book. You want to make a difference in your community and help shape a legacy that will last for generations. But you should always remember that what you're building isn't yours.

Yes, there can and should be coordination. Yes, there should be key leaders and changemakers.

But ownership? That belongs to the community.

When one entity tries to run everything and control the narrative, gatekeep the resources, dictate who gets invited in, etc., momentum dies. Trust erodes. Innovation slows.

The best ecosystems thrive when power is shared, communication is open, and credit is collective. When you are less concerned with whose name is on the plaque and more committed to generating community buy-in. And to accomplish that, multiple organizations can lead in different ways.

Think of yourself not as the hub but as an interconnected web of support organizations where information flows freely from one point to another without having to pass through a clearinghouse. Where no single entity is directing activity, but all are collaborating and sharing in the entrepreneur's journey. In their success.

3. Waiting for Permission

When some people hear Rear Admiral Grace Hopper's quote, "It's easier to ask for forgiveness than it is to get permission," they sometimes take it to mean they can act recklessly or without worrying about consequences. Do what you want and just apologize for it later. Not only is that not what she meant; it's also a powerful way to stifle collaboration and destroy trust.

No. That statement is about knowing when to do the right thing. It's about knowing when to push forward, even if you don't have explicit approval. It's about feeling empowered to advance the mission without having to wait for approval. In a collaborative ecosystem (just like a heavily bureaucratic environment like the U.S. Navy) with multiple stakeholders, if you have to get permission for everything, nothing will happen.

Entrepreneurship is a bottom-up force. It doesn't wait for government approval or a five-year strategic plan. It responds to need. It adapts. It moves fast and breaks assumptions.

So, if you're an ecosystem builder, don't wait for someone to give you the green light.

If you're a founder with an idea, don't wait for perfect conditions.

And if you're in city leadership? Sometimes the most powerful thing you can do is step back, listen, and remove the barriers in the way. Don't try to control the process. Create space for it to happen.

Innovation doesn't need a permission slip. It just needs room to breathe.

Building an ecosystem is hard enough without setting traps for yourself. Stay focused on people, not just programs. Share the mic. Share the credit. Move with urgency, and don't be afraid to lead from wherever you are.

Avoiding these pitfalls won't guarantee success.

But falling into them? That's almost always a fast track to stagnation.

Ecosystems Don't Happen to a City—They Happen Because of It

Creating a thriving startup ecosystem doesn't just happen.

They don't arrive with a ribbon-cutting for a new business incubator building.

They don't emerge from a single grant or strategic plan.

And they certainly don't happen just because someone hired a consultant or built a coworking space.

Ecosystems happen when people decide they're ready to build something bigger than themselves.

When founders, educators, city leaders, and everyday residents stop asking, "Why isn't someone doing this?" and start saying, "What can we do together?"

They happen when local colleges open their doors to students with ideas.

When nonprofits collaborate instead of compete.

When economic developers invest in long-term systems, not just short-term wins.

When risk-takers are celebrated not just when they succeed, but because they were bold enough to try.

And most of all, they happen when a city stops waiting for permission and starts taking ownership.

This work isn't easy. It requires showing up, again and again. It asks you to think strategically, systemically, intentionally, and collaboratively. It asks that you lead with humility and build with inclusivity. It's hard work, but it's also the most meaningful kind of work you can do because it has the power to transform not just businesses, but entire communities.

So, no, the question isn't, "Can a city like yours build a startup ecosystem?"

We already know the answer to that.

Cities from Chattanooga, TN, to Boise, ID, are proving it every day.

The real question is, "Are you willing to be part of it?"

Are you willing to do the hard, unglamorous, often invisible work that turns intention into infrastructure? Are you willing to build something that outlives you?

Because at the end of the day, ecosystems don't happen to a city. They happen because of it.

And the future belongs to those who are willing to build.

CHAPTER 2: MORE THAN JUST TECH AND TRENDS

"Commitment is what transforms a promise into reality."

-Abraham Lincoln, *16th President of the United States*

Most people think of a startup ecosystem as a place. They think of Austin or Silicon Valley. A city or a district with key components that help fuel entrepreneurial activity. Components like accelerators, venture capital, mentors, and service providers working in unison to support area entrepreneurs in starting and growing their businesses. While that may be technically correct, that's not where it starts.

It doesn't start with a flashy space, a pitch completion, or a training session. It begins with a promise. A promise that your city makes to entrepreneurs that they are not alone. That you're committing to their journey and to their eventual success.

A promise is between people. It's about relationships. Trust. Shared vision.

This is where small cities shine. Small cities are where personal connections are strong. Where community involvement runs deep. And where you can have a noticeable impact.

It's where creativity, compassion, and local grit are abundant and easy to find. You just have to know where to look.

It's the high school student testing an idea after class.

It's the retired engineer mentoring a young founder.

It's the city manager figuring out how to turn an underutilized warehouse into a shared innovation space.

It's the librarian hosting a coding bootcamp for young girls.

It's the local coffeeshop owner giving advice to their regulars.

It's the college professor encouraging a student to turn their side hustle into an exciting new business.

In small cities, a startup ecosystem is a living system rooted in relationships, driven by purpose, and sustained by belief. It's not just infrastructure. It's not just programming. It's a mindset, a culture, and a commitment to helping people turn ideas into impact.

And because it's so deeply intertwined with the identity of a place, small cities can't afford to copy someone else's blueprint. Remember, successful ecosystems are built off the assets around them. Different cities have different assets. What works in Seattle won't translate to Shreveport. What makes sense in Boston may fall flat in Brunswick.

That's why, in this chapter, we'll peel back the layers.

We'll define what a startup ecosystem really is, on your terms.

We'll explore the unique dynamics at play in smaller cities.

And we'll map out how to bring the essential ingredients (i.e., entrepreneurs, support systems, capital, talent, culture, and policy) together to form a cohesive, interconnected system that is uniquely yours.

Because when you stop chasing someone else's definition and start building a system that reflects your city's values, assets, and people, that is when things get real.

That's when momentum builds.

That's when ecosystems actually take root.

What an Ecosystem Can Be

Somewhere along the way, the term *startup ecosystem* got boxed in.

We began to treat it like a formula: something you could replicate by importing best practices from places like Austin or Palo Alto. If we just followed the same steps, we'd get the same results, right? Build an accelerator, host some pitch competitions, maybe throw in a tech hub and a TEDx or 1 Million Cups, and presto: ecosystem.

But here's the problem. Those places didn't start with a playbook. They didn't emerge from templates or toolkits. They started with people: people who saw problems worth solving, who gathered around a common purpose, and who refused to wait for someone else to fix it.

The heart of a real ecosystem isn't programming; it's possibility.

It's about building an environment where someone with an idea has the tools, the support, and the encouragement to turn that idea into something real.

And stick with it long enough to turn that venture into something valuable for themselves, their families, and their community.

A startup ecosystem is a culture that favors trying new things over getting things right. Where attempting and failing is part of the journey and not the end of it.

A vibrant ecosystem has resources that are easy to get to, mentors who listen, funders who take early bets, and programs that make the jargon easier to understand. There are community leaders who don't just talk about new ideas but also make it possible for others to take charge and policies that make things easier, less biased, and more open to involvement by everyone, not just the typical suspects.

A vibrant ecosystem has places that encourage working together, not merely occupying the same space. Places where people with amazing ideas come together and the energy of entrepreneurship proliferates.

But the connections made through an ecosystem are what really make it work, more than any physical area or program. I'm not talking about the kind of networking that focuses on "What can you do for me?" and is meant to help people do business. I'm talking about the kinds of connections that come from real relationships. The kinds of relationships that let people trust each other across departments. The kind that lasts longer than one event. The kind that gives someone the strength to keep going, even when things are tough.

That's what separates a program from a movement.

So, if you're building an ecosystem in your city, don't start with Silicon Valley in mind. Start with the people in front of you.

Ask what they need.

Listen to their dreams.

And then start building a system that reflects your city's own truth, not a copy of someone else's success.

A Living System, Not a Straight Line

You've all seen them. Nice roadmaps that outline the startup journey.

When should you validate an idea?

When should you set up your business?

When should you ask for funding?

These step-by-step maps appear helpful in that they are trying to use logic models to guide the entrepreneur in their journey. The problem is that in doing so, they make very broad generalizations. They assume that every entrepreneur walks the same path. That they walk down the same street.

In reality, if you're looking for a roadmap with mile markers and predictable turns, you're going to be disappointed because startup ecosystems don't develop like roads; they develop more like trails in the forest. Naturally. Unevenly. Organically. While roads are designed to counter the forces of nature, trails are designed to adapt to the environment and blend harmoniously with their surroundings.

And while we love tidy logic models and step-by-step guides, ecosystems rarely play by those rules. You can't just launch a new program, add some funding, host a few events, and assume you've built something that will last. That's not how this works.

Ecosystems are alive. And like any living system, they're complex, adaptive, and deeply relational. They're the bees that help spread pollen. The fallen log has now become a source of refuge. They are the small, quiet things that happen behind the scenes that help the ecosystem thrive.

And just like any ecosystem, startup ecosystems are full of quiet moments that make the system thrive. They are seen in the conversations and small moments that happen throughout your city. It's the moment a local high school principal agrees to host a pitch competition or when a chamber of commerce shifts its focus from ribbon cuttings to startup showcases. It's the moment a CEO and CFO sit to discuss local procurement processes or when a city council member finally sees entrepreneurship as more than just tech bros in hoodies.

None of that makes headlines because people, not programs, form the foundation of any ecosystem. Not just their titles or roles, but their willingness to work together, share ownership, and keep showing up even when the early results feel uncertain.

That's the hard part for many small cities. We've been taught to look for silver bullets: a new incubator, a fancy grant, a charismatic founder. But ecosystems aren't made in one bold move. They're made in a hundred quiet ones.

So give yourself permission to build patiently. Celebrate the unglamorous wins. Understand that some of the most vital changes won't be visible until long after they've taken root.

Because the goal isn't simply to follow a straight line.

It's to grow something resilient, real, and rooted in your community. Something that lasts.

Small Cities, Custom Ecosystems

If there's one message I want small cities to take to heart, it's that you don't have to look like anyone else to build a thriving startup ecosystem. In fact, if your city is just trying to copy Austin's culture or Boulder's blueprint, you're missing the point entirely.

The most resilient ecosystems aren't replicas; they're reflections of its people, of its culture.

Take a rural county where broadband is patchy and there's no formal incubator in sight. That doesn't mean you're out of the game. Maybe what you do have is a deeply connected network of churches, faith-based organizations, and community centers where trust runs deep. That's infrastructure. That's convening power. Use it. Turn fellowship halls into makerspaces. Invite congregants to share business ideas after service. Build your ecosystem around relationships that already exist.

Or maybe your city is home to a vibrant immigrant community, with people running pop-up restaurants from their kitchens, selling hand-crafted goods on weekends, and repairing appliances out of garages. That's not informal hustle; it's entrepreneurial energy. Don't try to "formalize" it by forcing it into rigid startup programs designed for Silicon Valley. Instead, make pathways that are adaptable and take into account culture, language, and lived experience. Provide micro-capital, mentorship in native languages, and ad support to amplify their story. Empower what's already working.

And if you live in an area where the local trade school is turning out welders, electricians, and diesel mechanics, don't ignore them simply because they don't wear lab coats or know how to code. These are skilled workers who are good at solving problems and typically want to start their own businesses. What if we thought of them as possible founders? What if we established an environment that valued blue-collar creativity as much as software development?

Remember that every community has assets. The work of building an ecosystem isn't about importing shiny solutions from somewhere else. It's about surfacing the hidden strengths already living in your city and designing around those.

Don't wait for permission. Don't apologize for not being a tech hub. Don't try to retrofit someone else's strategy into your context.

Start with what's real. Start with what's local. Start with what you have. The best ecosystems aren't born from imitation; they're built from identity.

Everything's Better in Metter – Real World Example

When you drive into Metter, Georgia, you're greeted by a sign that reads, "Everything's Better in Metter." It's a bold claim for a rural community of just over 4,000 people, but if you've spent any time there and walked its downtown, shaken hands with its entrepreneurs, or seen the pride in the eyes of its farmers, you'll start to believe it.

A few years ago, Mandi was still in her honeymoon period as the new city manager. She'd seen what we'd done elsewhere and saw it as an opportunity to help Metter differentiate itself from other rural communities in the state. After a series of conversations, we agreed to assess the community's assets through a series of community-wide forums and a feasibility study. We performed a deep dive into the community's assets and looked at everything, not just the pretty parts.

What was clear was that the lack of density was going to be a barrier, but not an insurmountable one. To make something work, they were going to have to think more broadly. They were going to have to focus on developing an ecosystem—finding the right anchors that could help give their ecosystem meaning and the right place to give these conversations a home. And they were going to have to find a champion. Someone who could be the face of the effort and convene partners.

It didn't take long for Heidi to step into that role. She was serving as their downtown development director and jumped at the chance to serve both roles. Her passion for the community and the drive to make a difference quickly opened doors, not just in the city but throughout the state.

An old public works facility was quickly renovated with funding support from the state. Georgia Southern University stepped in to operate the incubator in the front of the building. And a startup hydroponic company that was just getting off the ground elsewhere agreed to call Metter home.

Shortly thereafter, the Georgia Department of Agriculture's marketing division, called Georgia Grown, committed to making resources, such as promotion support, training, and networking opportunities, available to incubator clients. In no time, the facility was rebranded, and the Georgia Grown Innovation Center (GGIC) was born.

What makes GGIC remarkable isn't just the infrastructure; it's the intentionality. This wasn't a "build it and they will come" project. This is a "build it and walk alongside them" philosophy. Entrepreneurs don't just come here for space; they come for resources. They come for market research, branding expertise, and connections to the Georgia Grown network.

One of my favorite stories from GGIC involves Mattie and Curtis and EKC Farms. When they first came to GGIC, they had 800 pecan trees to tend and harvest. Their goal was to seek help and guidance to sustain the farm that has been in their family for generations. What they got was more than just guidance. With the help of a university design professor and his students, they got rebranded packaging. With the help of a regional nonprofit wholesale distributor, they got their pecans placed in grocery stores throughout the Southeast. And with the help of public broadcasting, they got their story blasted throughout the state.

And what the community got in return was belief. Belief not just in Mattie and Curtis, but belief that entrepreneurs in this small town had a product worth buying and a story worth telling.

That's the magic of the GGIC. It's not trying to turn Metter into the next Austin or Boulder. It's trying to make Metter the best version of itself. A place where agricultural heritage meets modern market opportunity. In doing so, it's proving that innovation doesn't just happen in big cities. It happens wherever people have the courage to dream and the support to execute.

Metter's Georgia Grown Innovation Center is a reminder to every rural community that your ideas are worth investing in, your products can compete on a national stage, and your future can be as bold as the sign that greets visitors on the edge of town.

That's what you're building when you tell stories with heart and intention. Not just visibility. Belief.

Action Checklist: Understanding and Defining Your Ecosystem

Before you can build your startup ecosystem, you have to see it.

Not imagine it. Not import it. Not wish it into existence.

You just have to see it, clearly and honestly, for what it is today. That means pulling back the curtain on what's really happening in your city, not just what's showing up in grant reports or glossy brochures.

Here are a few things you can do to help you get started:

Map Your Local Assets—Formal and Informal

- Don't just list incubators and coworking spaces. Think broader. Where are people already gathering? Where is trust already established? That neighborhood barber who knows every young hustler in town; that's an asset. That community garden where retirees swap stories and ideas; that's an asset. Look beyond the obvious.

Identify Who's Already Supporting Entrepreneurs—Even Unofficially

- Some supporters are easy to spot. Your local SBDC or SCORE chapter. The entrepreneurship center at your university. But others may be a bit more difficult to identify. It might be the woman running a daycare out of her home who's quietly mentoring others. Or the retired banker who helps neighbors apply for loans. Or the church group helping members turn side gigs into businesses. These "under-the-radar" champions often do more to fuel entrepreneurship than any formal office.

Convene Diverse Voices

- When you're just getting started, it's easy to lean on a few people. You want positive energy, and you want to move quickly. But don't let your ecosystem become a clique. Don't rely on the same insiders that know all the key players and everyone seems to know. Bring in the barbers, bakers, mechanics, side-hustling teachers, nonprofit leaders, and first-time founders. Innovation is happening in every corner of your community. You just have to invite it into the conversation.

Define Your Own Ecosystem Goals Based on Local Needs

- Are you trying to reduce brain drain? Create jobs that don't rely on recruitment from outside? Turn informal businesses into formal ones? Support second-career founders? Don't adopt someone else's metrics. Build goals that reflect your city's aspirations, and build metrics around your goals.

Anchor Your Efforts in Relationships, Not Just Resources

- While access to capital is important, trust is far more valuable. And trust builds faster than capital. If your founders don't feel connected to mentors, peers, and champions, no amount of funding will create real momentum. Relationships are the connective tissue of an ecosystem. Invest in them early and often.

Prioritize Inclusion From the Very Beginning

- If you want an equitable ecosystem, you can't retrofit equity later. Make space for the voices, leaders, and communities who have historically been left out of "innovation" conversations. True ecosystems grow stronger when *everyone* can see themselves as a builder.

If You Can See the System, You Can Shape It

When you look at established ecosystems, it's easy to marvel at how smoothly everything runs. The linkages between programs seem obvious, and the handoff between support organizations seems effortless. But startup ecosystems often exist in fragments. They're hidden in back rooms, after-school programs, lunch counters, and late-night side hustles. But when you take the time to name the system, when you map the players, channel the energy, identify the gaps, and appreciate the strengths, you unlock something powerful.

Visibility Creates Momentum

Once people begin to see themselves as part of a larger vision, they show up differently. They speak up. They collaborate. They invest. They buy in.

You don't have to manufacture a startup scene from scratch.

You don't need millions in funding to get started.

You simply need to recognize what's *already* growing in your community—and give it the space, support, and sunlight it needs to thrive.

Because when a small city truly believes it can shape its own economic future, it becomes unstoppable.

And that's when the real work begins.

PART II

LAYING THE FOUNDATION

CHAPTER 3:
ASSESSING YOUR CITY'S READINESS

"When we look in the mirror, we should focus on our potential, not our limitations."

-Nelson Mandela, *Long Walk to Freedom*

Before any small city can hope to become the next Boulder, Austin, or Chattanooga, it has to stop, slow down, and look itself squarely in the mirror.

Not through the lens of a grant application.

Not filtered through a flashy consulting report.

Not by checking someone else's boxes for what innovation should look like.

But through an honest, unflinching self-assessment of who you really are. Your DNA, your people, your assets, and your blind spots.

When I first began collaborating with communities to promote entrepreneurship, it seemed as though everyone was eager to open an incubator or launch something like a pitch competition, a tech hub, or a "Shark Tank"-style event. But few had done the hard work of asking:

- What are we actually working with?

- Do we even have the right soil for something meaningful to grow?

- Are we planting seeds or pulling weeds?

Often the catalyst for these conversations was a vacant downtown building that they believed would make the perfect entrepreneurship hub. They would speak with excitement of the structure of the facility, its prime location, and the endless possibilities that lie between its walls. They would have a *Field of Dreams* moment. They believed that "if you build it, they will come."

I have to admit, these were exciting conversations to have. Imagination would run deep, the energy would be contagious, and the possibilities would be endless. All they had to do was "build it," and the entrepreneurs would come from the fields to build the next great company, and the students would stay in their city to work in these exciting new jobs.

The energy would always pause when I started to ask, "Where are the investors?"

"Why aren't the students staying?"

"Why aren't we attracting tech talent?"

It's always challenging to balance early enthusiasm with processes designed to assess and uncover underlying motivations and frustrations. But this is no different than having an entrepreneur so excited about their new product that they overlook crucial steps, such as customer discovery or market assessment.

These steps help get an unfiltered view of who you are. Start with an assessment of local trends, demographics, retail, manufacturing, and industrial activities. Look at the strength of your technical core. The availability of key assets, such as anchor institutions, as well as support organizations like the SBDC and SCORE. Do they have the capacity for growth? Are they willing to help build something great in your community?

A proper assessment can help you gauge your city's assets and understand who you are. It can present a clear picture of your strengths but also the challenges that lie ahead.

Supplement that with focus groups. Think of these as opportunities to do a deep dive into the community culture. An opportunity to discover things about the city that you can't tell from the data. Ask:

- Do we have a culture that supports risk-taking?

- Do entrepreneurs feel visible and valued?

- Are our support systems coordinated or chaotic?

- Do our policies make it easier or harder to start something new?

Use this process to not only help galvanize the community but also to test stakeholder commitment. When done right, this becomes less about a feasibility study or community assessment or what a consultant said you should do. It's about unlocking your community's desire for growth. It focuses on assessing the community's willingness to embrace change and its dedication to the challenging task of building a startup ecosystem. Because startup ecosystems aren't transplanted. They're grown. And growth only happens when you prepare the ground.

Why This Work Matters

Diagnostic work isn't sexy. It doesn't make headlines.

You won't get standing ovations for hosting a listening session or mapping your city's hidden networks.

But without it, everything else is just posturing. Just theater.

Ecosystem building isn't about copying someone else's model. It's about building your own from the inside out. That means:

- Knowing which assets are dormant but full of potential;

- Seeing where trust has been eroded and committing to repair it;

- Identifying your community's "unofficial" leaders and pulling them into the conversation;

- Naming what's missing, not to assign blame, but to create alignment.

The Real Test of Readiness

Michael Jackson may have been talking about ecosystem building when he sang about looking inward to affect the type of change that you want to see in the world in his song, "The Man in the Mirror."

As an ecosystem builder, you have to look at yourself in the mirror and ask, "Are you willing to let go of ego and embrace honesty?"

"Can your community move beyond wishful thinking and into purposeful action?"

Because the truth is, every small city has something. A hidden advantage. A tight-knit network. A deep reservoir of hustle. But that "something" only becomes powerful when it's recognized, respected, and aligned with intent.

This chapter is about helping you uncover that truth clearly, courageously, and without shortcuts because before you build your startup ecosystem, you need to understand the ecosystem that already exists.

It's not glamorous work. But it's the foundation everything else depends on.

And in my experience, the communities that commit to this kind of intentional and honest reflection are the ones that go the farthest the fastest.

So: look in the mirror.

Not to judge, but to understand.

Not to copy others, but to discover who you can become.

Step 1: Identify What You Already Have

Before you grow anything new, you have to take inventory of what's already in the ground.

Too often, small cities assume they're "starting from scratch" because they don't see incubators, startup funds, or unicorn founders walking around. But ecosystems aren't just built on buzzwords or branded spaces. They're built on people, places, and programs that are already working, whether or not they carry the label of "entrepreneurship."

That means you're probably more equipped than you think.

You just have to know where and how to look.

Start With an Asset Inventory

Every ecosystem starts with assets. But in small cities, they don't always show up where you expect them. Forget the Silicon Valley scorecard. What you're looking for is function, not form.

Here's a simple framework to begin:

People

Start with the doers and the connectors. Who has experience starting or running businesses? Who mentors others, formally or informally? Who's the retired bank manager that still meets with young entrepreneurs over coffee? Who's organizing the monthly side-hustle meetups in their church basement?

- Look for creators, funders, champions, and bridge-builders.

- Don't just focus on people with titles. Focus on people with influence.

Institutions

Local institutions are your scaffolding. These might include:

- Colleges and universities with small business centers or entrepreneurship minors;

- K–12 schools with robotic clubs or innovation programs;

- Nonprofits and civic groups doing leadership development, youth engagement, or workforce training;

- Chambers of commerce or local development authorities with convening power.

The key question isn't what they call themselves; it's what role could they play?

Spaces

You don't need a shiny tech hub in the middle of town to encourage new ideas. Look for venues where people already meet and work together:

- Libraries that have rooms for meetings;

- Buildings that aren't being used enough that could be turned into coworking or makerspaces;

- Media centers in high schools, church halls, or even coffee shops that people like.

Be imaginative with how you use space. Just remember that being close to someone helps you connect with them.

Programs

You might already have initiatives that help people start their own businesses without calling them that. Check for:

- Competitions for businesses, especially those for young people and minorities;

- Classes on new ideas or startup weekends at schools in the area;

- Grants for workforce development that could be used to teach people how to start their own businesses;

- Civic engagement initiatives or leadership groups that teach people how to think like an entrepreneur.

> ## Bonus Tip: Don't Forget About Informal Networks
>
> In small markets, informal networks are often more powerful than formal ones. It is through these hidden conversations, like when a hairstylist refers clients to a friend's Etsy store or when a youth pastor encourages young members to start side hustles, that your ecosystem can really take off. These people may not show up on an organizational chart, but they're often the glue holding your ecosystem together.
>
> So ask yourself:
>
> - Who do people call when they need help launching something?
>
> - Who's already trusted by the community and could help widen the circle?

You're Not Starting From Zero

The goal of Step 1 isn't just to fill out a spreadsheet. It's to shift your perspective.

Remember, you're not trying to invent a startup ecosystem from scratch.

You're trying to uncover what already exists and organize it with purpose.

The raw materials are likely already in your community. The real challenge is naming them, connecting them, and activating them in a way that aligns with your local identity and goals.

And once you start seeing those assets for what they are, you'll realize that you're further along than you thought.

Step 2: Acknowledge the Gaps

This is the step most communities want to skip and exactly the one they can't afford to.

Every city has gaps. That's not a sign of failure. It's a sign you're paying attention.

But naming those gaps? That takes courage. Because once you see them, you have to decide what you're going to do about them. Are you going to ignore them, or are you willing to do the real work of addressing them?

I've worked with many small towns with sparkling new innovation hubs that sat mostly empty. Not because people didn't care, but because the ecosystem didn't yet have a pipeline of entrepreneurs ready to fill the space.

So before we pour more concrete or print more pitch decks, we have to ask:

What's truly missing?

And even more critically, what's holding us back culturally?

Common Gaps in Small City Ecosystems

If you look close enough, you'll probably notice certain gaps in your community. Here are five of the most common and most consequential gaps that I consistently come across:

1. No unified narrative

There's no clear or shared story around entrepreneurship.

People don't know who's doing what.

Founders don't feel celebrated.

The community doesn't yet see entrepreneurship as part of its identity.

If people can't tell the story of your ecosystem, it becomes invisible, even to the people building it.

2. Lack of early-stage capital

Especially in the crucial under-$50,000 range.

This isn't about venture capital. It's about friends-and-family rounds that don't exist for many founders.

Without early cash, promising ideas stay stuck in notebooks. Inclusion starts with access, and access starts with affordability.

3. Siloed support efforts

Everyone wants to run a pitch competition or offer mentoring services. The problem is that you've got three organizations doing similar things, and no one is talking to each other.

No shared referral system. No common goals. Lots of duplicated effort, little collective momentum.

When it comes to ecosystem building, coordination beats competition every time.

4. Youth disengagement

In many cities, not just small ones, students simply don't see entrepreneurship as a path for them.

Local schools aren't connected to startup activity.

Young talent leaves because they don't see opportunity in staying, and those that do stay feel left behind.

If your ecosystem doesn't excite the next generation, it's not built to last.

5. No ecosystem lead

No one wakes up every day thinking about the big picture.

You may have a lot of great people doing good work, but no one is stitching it together.

Without a convener, even the best intentions drift apart.

Ecosystems don't need a CEO. But they do need a gardener. Someone to tend the system, connect the dots, and ensure the whole is greater than the sum of its parts.

The Harder Question: What's Holding Us Back Culturally?

Sometimes the real barriers aren't technical. They're cultural.

- Is failure seen as shameful?

- Are certain voices consistently left out of the conversation?

- Is there an "old guard" resistant to new ideas or new leadership?

- Do we treat entrepreneurship like a side hobby rather than a career path?

- Is the ecosystem built for all or just for a few?

Culture is the undercurrent of every ecosystem. You can have the right programs on paper, but if the community culture discourages risk-taking, undervalues local founders, or resists collaboration, your momentum will stall.

As you build your ecosystem, it is important to reflect on the culture that you have in place. The next time you convene your ecosystem roundtable or strategy session, ask these questions:

- What parts of our ecosystem feel disconnected?

- Where are we duplicating efforts instead of coordinating?

- Who's not at the table but should be?

- What stories are we telling about entrepreneurship in this city?

- Who's waking up every day with this work on their mind?

Gaps Aren't the Problem. Silence Is

Don't be afraid of what's missing. Be afraid of pretending everything's already in place.

Because once you name the gaps, you give your community permission to close them—together.

And that's how real ecosystems grow: by being honest, inclusive, and relentless in the pursuit of something better. Not by hiding their gaps.

Step 3: Map the Players and Their Roles

If Step 1 is about taking inventory and Step 2 is about owning the gaps, then Step 3 is where you begin to put the puzzle together. And when I say "you," I mean all of you.

That's because you can't build a startup city alone. And more importantly, you shouldn't.

Ecosystems thrive, not when one organization does everything, but when everyone knows what they do best and how it fits into the bigger picture.

This is the alignment phase. And it starts by getting clear on who's at the table and what seat they actually occupy.

Think of This Like Casting a Community-Wide Play

Every ecosystem needs actors, stagehands, directors, and promoters.

You've got people working behind the scenes and people in the spotlight.

What matters isn't the title. It's the function.

Take a look around and ask yourself:

- Who's creating opportunities?

- Who's convening the players?

- Who's funding the action?

- Who's telling the story?

- Who's supporting the talent?

- Who's building the stage?

When everyone knows their role and respects the roles of others, momentum becomes manageable.

But when roles are unclear, you get duplicated efforts, stepped-on toes, frustrated players, and missed opportunities.

Core Roles in a Thriving Ecosystem

In Chapter 1, we defined the core components of a startup ecosystem to include entrepreneurs, support organizations, capital, talent, culture, and policy. Their inclusion is important to helping develop and sustain your ecosystem. Now, we are describing the roles that key individuals and institutions play in building and maintaining your ecosystem. To help you understand who they are and why they are needed, I have listed the common archetypes you'll find in most startup ecosystems. You might already know some of these people in your area.

- **The founders**

  The heart of your ecosystem. They construct, test, fail, change direction, and inspire. Nothing else matters without them.

- **The educators**

  Professors, teachers, and people who train workers. They help develop local talent and get people thinking like entrepreneurs at a young age.

- **The connectors**

  Leaders of chambers of commerce, community activists, and others with power in the area. These are the people who will connect the dots between different groups and keep the conversation going.

- **The builders**

  Accelerators, incubators, university centers, and initiatives run by nonprofits. They give early-stage businesses the structure, training, and help they need.

- **The funders**

  Bankers, angel investors, grant producers, and community development finance institutions (CDFIs). They will help turn ideas into action by making money available.

- **The storytellers**

  Local reporters, podcasters, and people who run social media. These are the folks who will change the story, make the voice louder, and show what startups are doing.

- **The policymakers**

  People who work for the city, such as elected politicians, municipal planners, and economic developers. They are in charge of the infrastructure investments, zoning regulations, incentive structures, and procurement policy.

- **The anchors**

  Hospitals, colleges, factories, utilities, and so on. These are the biggest companies that hire people and buy things in your area. How they get goods and services and hire people can have a direct effect on whether a startup stays in business.

- The ecosystem stewards

Every day, someone (or a small group) works to keep the system healthy. They don't own the ecosystem, but they water, care for, and connect it.

Build a Visual Map

Occasionally, the clearest way to define roles is to literally draw them. Try this exercise with your local team:

1. List every organization involved in providing entrepreneurship support, even those loosely connected.

2. Categorize them based on function, not form(Is this group providing capital? Connections? Capacity building?)

3. Identify gaps. Are any roles missing entirely?

4. Clarify overlaps. Are multiple groups playing the same part? Can they coordinate?

Clearly understanding who everyone is, what they are doing, and what role they are playing, as well as who's missing, can add a great deal of clarity to the effort.

Avoid Role Confusion

One of the biggest threats to healthy ecosystems is organizations not knowing where they fit or trying to do everything.

You don't need every organization to be an accelerator. You need each to play their role well.

Remember that clarity breeds collaboration.

When everyone knows their lane and how it connects to others, the whole system moves faster, smoother, and with more trust.

Shared Purpose, Distinct Roles

Startups succeed because great teams align around a shared mission, an organizational culture, and a clear go-to-market strategy. Startup cities are no different.

It starts by knowing who you are and what you're selling. So get clear. Get honest. Get aligned.

And when you do? You'll stop just talking about ecosystem building and start living it.

CHAPTER 4:
CREATING A UNIFIED VISION AND LEADERSHIP TEAM

"If you are working on something exciting that you really care about, you don't have to be pushed. The vision pulls you."

-Steve Jobs, *co-founder, Apple, Inc.*

Who's in Charge?

There I stood in a room full of passionate community leaders to discuss creating a new entrepreneurship hub in the center of town. The CEO of the chamber of commerce had invited me to share my experiences in a similar community located approximately an hour east. The enthusiasm was evident right from the start. They were just as eager to hear about my trials as they were about my successes.

We discussed the early challenges of building an ecosystem and the cumbersome tasks of maintaining buy-in. We discussed the roles of the people in the room, beyond their day jobs but within the ecosystem. And we spoke of the possible involvement of anchor institutions. But as the conversation shifted from "what could be" to "how do we," I noticed the energy shift from near childlike enthusiasm to slight apprehension. A telling moment was when one of the chamber board members asked a seemingly simple question, "So… who's going to be in charge of this thing?"

As the others in the room looked slightly perplexed, I couldn't contain my enthusiasm. After a near-hour-long discussion of purpose and possibilities, the question of ownership was in the air. The fact that they'd even asked this question meant they care. It meant they were ready to move from abstract conversations to real coordination.

Ecosystems Are Not Programs; They're Not Departments

While the chamber leaders were quick to recognize the endless possibilities of building a startup ecosystem in their community, they had not yet realized that you can't assign an ecosystem to a single organization and expect it to thrive. You can't run it like a grant-funded project and think it will outlast the money. And you definitely can't outsource it to a task force that meets quarterly and calls it collaboration.

A startup ecosystem is not:

- A nonprofit;
- A university initiative;
- A mayor's pet project;

- A one-year campaign;

- A branded hub with a logo and a website.

It's not something that a chamber can own. In fact, the more identifiable it is with one organization, the more fragile it is.

An Ecosystem Is a Network

And networks thrive under a different logic.

Networks are not about ownership or the strength of a single node. They're about distributive information and shared contacts. As such, they thrive when:

- Vision is shared, not owned;

- Leadership is distributed, not concentrated;

- Structure supports, but doesn't suffocate;

- Trust flows horizontally, not just top-down.

This is why developing a strong ecosystem is so challenging. You need just enough structure to create alignment but not so much that you choke the grassroots energy that makes startups work in the first place.

What Does Leadership Look Like in a Healthy Ecosystem?

It looks more like a coalition than a chain of command. It's less about control and more about cultivation. The most resilient ecosystems I've seen are ones where:

- Universities, economic developers, founders, and nonprofits are all in regular conversation;

- No one has to ask permission to try something new;

- There's a clear backbone organization or convener but also enough autonomy for others to lead;

- Leaders prioritize collective impact over individual credit.

In building a startup ecosystem, you don't need a boss, but you do need a backbone. Every ecosystem benefits from a neutral convener, someone (or a small team) waking up every day thinking about the health of the whole system.

But this backbone entity isn't the owner.

They don't dictate direction.

Their job is to connect, translate, coordinate, and catalyze. They keep conversations going, spot duplication, and encourage alignment. Equally, they work to ensure inclusion, especially of voices that aren't usually invited to the table. And they keep the flywheel spinning even when attention wavers.

This Chapter Is About Building That Alignment

It's about getting the right people in the room and helping them see that they're not competitors. They're collaborators in a shared system.

It's about naming roles, mapping relationships, and designing governance that works for your city, not just copying what another community did.

It's about balancing the energy of "move fast and break things" with the wisdom of "move together and build something that will endure."

Momentum starts to show up when you transition from scattered efforts to shared alignment. Not just in headlines, but in lives changed, businesses launched, and communities transformed.

Start with a Clear, Community-Driven Vision

If you want a thriving startup ecosystem, you need more than momentum. You need a North Star—a vision that's not just catchy but anchored in place, rooted in people, and committed to outcomes that matter.

The vision needs to embody who you are and where you are going.

"We want to be the next Silicon Valley" is not a vision. It's an aspiration wrapped in a buzzword. And worse, it signals that a community is chasing someone else's success story rather than owning its own.

You can't borrow someone else's identity and expect to build something authentic. The vision can't be imported or imposed.

What a Real Vision Looks Like

A real, grounded ecosystem vision reflects three things:

1. Your City's Identity

Not just what it is now, but what it has been and what it hopes to become.

- What are your historical industries?

- What's the cultural heartbeat of your community?

- What legacy are you carrying forward?

2. Your Unique Value Proposition

What do you offer that larger innovation hubs can't?

- Is it your density of relationships?

- Your affordability and quality of life?

- Your tradition of craftsmanship, grit, or creativity?

- Your access to certain anchor institutions?

3. Your Community's Priorities

A vision isn't visionary if it doesn't serve the people who live there.

- Are you trying to retain local talent?

- Create pathways for underrepresented entrepreneurs?

- Diversify a stagnant economy or revitalize downtown?

A Working Example

A strong, grounded ecosystem vision might say something like:

"To make [City Name] a place where anyone with an idea and determination can start and grow a business that is supported by a collaborative network of local institutions, mentors, and champions committed to providing inclusive economic opportunity."

If your ecosystem speaks more to creatives, you may want to emphasize "a place where creative businesses and individuals can thrive." If your focus is on a specific sector or subsector, like health care, mobility, or agribusiness, don't hesitate to embrace it. You must be specific and develop something that is actionable.

And most importantly, it needs to feel like something that could only be said about your community.

The Process Is the Point

How you craft the vision matters just as much as what it says. It isn't something you do in isolation or outsource to a marketing consultant. This isn't branding. It's trust-building.

Too many well-meaning leaders write a vision statement in a boardroom and then try to "roll it out" to the community. But if you didn't build it with them, don't expect people to buy into it.

You want a vision that lasts? Build it the right way:

- Host roundtables that include founders, students, artists, and faith leaders, not just the usual suspects.

- Do surveys in multiple languages and formats, not just online.

- Go where people already gather—community centers, barber shops, and farmers markets.

- Listen more than you talk.

The outcome isn't just a document. It's a shared sense of ownership. And that ownership is what sustains the ecosystem when the momentum stalls and the initial energy fades.

The Vision Sets the Standard

Once you have outlined your vision statement, it becomes your filter for how your ecosystem operates. It will serve as your efforts' North Star and help you reflect on actions:

- Does this program align with our values?

- Is this partnership inclusive of our whole community?

- Are we chasing funding that pulls us off course or moving toward what we said we'd build?

A clear, community-driven vision doesn't just point the way forward. It keeps you honest. Because in the end, a startup ecosystem encompasses more than just entrepreneurship. It's about taking actions that help shape the community. And the clearer your community is about what it wants to become, the more power it has to shape that future.

Identify and Empower Your Core Leadership Team

As much as we'd like this to be true, startup ecosystems don't build themselves. They require a collective effort and community-wide buy-in. No single person, no matter how passionate, well-connected, and visionary, can carry the weight of the whole system on their shoulders.

What you need is a core group of stewards, people committed to the service of the ecosystem. A dedicated coalition of individuals that wake up every day thinking not just about their own organizations, but about the health of the entire ecosystem.

Think of this group as your Ecosystem Stewardship Team.

Why This Team Matters

In any system, a committed and aligned leadership team makes the difference between momentum and fragmentation. Without clear alignment, your efforts become scattered, programs overlap, and energy dissipates. With it, you get cohesion, accountability, and shared purpose.

An Ecosystem Stewardship Team isn't about command and control or putting in place a hierarchy to direct activities. It's about commitment.

These are your connectors, your navigators, and your builders of trust and bridges.

They're the ones who will keep the flywheel turning, name the gaps in your system, and hold the long-term vision when short-term distractions flare up. But this only works if you choose the right people and give them real authority to act.

Who Should Be at the Table

An effective Ecosystem Stewardship Team is cross-sector, community-rooted, and entrepreneur-centered. When developing your team, I encourage you to start with the people already filling the core roles that you identified in the previous chapter. Whenever possible, it should include members from all relevant sectors.

Local Government: Leaders who can align public policy to encourage growth, open up funding streams, and remove bureaucratic barriers. Look beyond just economic developers and consider planners, procurement officers, and even zoning staff. Think: enablers, not gatekeepers.

Higher Education: Champions from universities, technical colleges, and workforce programs. These institutions help shape talent pipelines, promote research commercialization, and provide legitimacy to entrepreneurial education.Think: bridges between theory and practice.

The Business Community: Established business owners, employers, and angel investors who bring not only capital but also credibility. They often know how to navigate local systems and where to find the hidden talent.Think: mentors, models, and multipliers.

Nonprofits & Economic Development Organizations: From chambers of commerce to Main Street programs to workforce boards, these are the organizations already embedded in community life. They understand how to convene, communicate, and catalyze action.

Think: boots on the ground with systems know-how.

Entrepreneurs: The importance of the entrepreneur cannot be overstated. If you don't have at least one active founder at the table, you don't have an ecosystem team. You have a committee. Entrepreneurs bring the lived experience. They keep the group grounded. They'll remind you that what sounds good in a white paper might not actually work in a coworking space at midnight.

Don't Just Invite—Empower

It's not enough to put names on a slide and call it a leadership team. People have to know what's being asked of them. They also need to know where they are headed and have the freedom to help shape the destination. To accomplish this, you have to take action.

- **Clarify roles and responsibilities.** Who's doing what? Who owns the follow-up? Who communicates with whom?**Build shared language and trust.** Hold regular meetings that are action-oriented, not performative. Create space for disagreement, but be sure to anchor it in shared values.**Distribute decision-making.** Avoid

> bottlenecks. Encourage co-leadership. Allow teams to experiment and adapt in real time.
>
> - **Measure collective impact.** Focus on system health, not just individual wins. Track relationship-building, information flow, and support gaps as seriously as you would new business starts.

Always keep in mind that the best ecosystems are not run by any single person or entity. They're held together by distributed leadership, shared stewardship, and a deep respect for lived experience.

Your Ecosystem Stewardship Team should reflect your entire community and not just the loudest voices or the most resourced institutions. The doers, the dreamers, and the people who've been quietly doing this work long before it was called "ecosystem building" should also be in the room. Because in the end, this isn't about who's in charge. It's about who's committed and who's showing up for the long haul.

Define Roles, Not Just Titles

Scottish philosopher Thomas Reid said, "There is no greater impediment to the advancement of knowledge than the ambiguity of words." While ambiguity can be a strategic advantage for entrepreneurs because it can help foster innovation and adaptability, when it comes to ecosystem building, it can be problematic. Ambiguity in roles, processes, and purpose can be the enemy of execution.

Too many well-intentioned efforts fizzle out, not because the idea lacked merit or the people lacked passion, but because no one really knew who was doing what.

I see it all the time. A dozen stakeholders in the room. Everyone nodding along. Lots of enthusiasm. Great energy.

And then?

Nothing happens. Why? Because "collaboration" without clear roles and expectations lacks the ability to hold people accountable. And a lack of accountability is a lack of results.

When Everyone's Responsible… No One Is

In ecosystem work, there's a dangerous myth: because the work is collaborative, everyone can just organically figure it out together. That shared vision alone will carry the day. But while ecosystems may be collaborative, they still need clarity.

You can have the most diverse, passionate, well-resourced group in the world, but if no one knows who's accountable for follow-up, coordination, or outcomes, the system will stall.

It's not enough to know who's at the table. You have to know why they're there and what they're responsible for.

Clarify Functions, Not Just Titles

Just because someone's title says "director," "coordinator," or "chief of staff" doesn't mean they're the right person to lead a certain initiative. And just because someone doesn't have an official title doesn't mean they're not already playing a critical role in the ecosystem.

Instead of defaulting to hierarchy or job descriptions, start by mapping the functions that your ecosystem needs filled.

For example:

- Champion—Keeps this work visible for funders, policymakers, and the media;

- Convener—Brings people together consistently and with purpose;

- Connector—Identifies gaps, bridges silos, and makes introductions between unlikely allies;

- Programmer—Designs programs and runs key initiatives;

- Communicator—Tells the story, both internally and externally, and promotes the ecosystem brand;

- Tracker—Tracks the metrics and evaluates the impact.

Take a look at who's currently providing each function, and don't be afraid to assess their effectiveness. Is it the right person? Do they have the authority and support to do it well? Could our ecosystem be better served if someone else operated in that capacity?

Put It in Writing

Once you've identified the key functions, document them. Instead of creating a 50-page manual, use a living guide that the Ecosystem Stewardship Team revisits regularly.

- Be explicit.

- Assign names.

- Set timelines.

The purpose isn't to create a bureaucracy. It's about alignment and accountability. You want to keep the structure loose so that the team can adapt swiftly to new information and feel empowered to take initiative.

At the same time, you want your leadership team to stay focused and on point. That's why it's important to clearly define their roles and to set a clear schedule. Because a loosely organized group of ecosystem champions with clearly defined roles will always outperform a tightly structured committee with vague intentions.

Shared Vision Requires Shared Responsibility

Having a shared vision and common goal is crucial, but it's equally important to take ownership of your part of the puzzle. Ecosystem building is messy, nonlinear, and relational. But that doesn't mean it should be leaderless or vague.

Some people are afraid that clarifying roles will place guardrails on the process and somehow kill creativity. But that couldn't be further from the truth. In fact, clarity is what allows creativity to thrive. Once people know where they fit and how to contribute, they begin to feel empowered to act.

So the next time your ecosystem effort kicks off a big initiative, don't just ask, "Who wants to be involved?"

Instead, ask the same question that was asked of me in the chamber boardroom, "Who's leading this and how will we know they're succeeding?"

That single question could be the difference between momentum and mediocrity.

Build Alignment, Not Uniformity

If you're reading this from the lens of a government official, university administrator, business leader, or entrepreneur, there's probably a part of you that wants to build something similar to what you're accustomed to. An organized structure, with a clear person in charge. But you're not building something like where you work. You're building a movement.

In startup ecosystem development, especially in small cities, it's tempting to look for a single, central leader. A keystone institution that controls the process. But that's not how ecosystems grow. That's how bureaucracies get built.

The Goal Isn't Consensus. It's Cohesion.

You don't need everyone to agree on every decision or follow the same playbook. In fact, if you're doing this right, you'll have tension. That's part of innovation.

And while you don't need unilateral agreement, you do need a shared framework. A framework that includes:

- A common vision—a North Star that everyone's aligned around;

- A shared understanding of roles—who's doing what and how it fits together;

- And perhaps most critically: a foundation of values that govern how you work.

Establishing a clear framework also enables your Ecosystem Stewardship Team to prioritize transparency, because everyone knows everyone else's roles and responsibilities. They are clear about the vision and know how everything is supposed to fit together. This transparency has the added benefit of mitigating turf wars.

Alignment Is an Ongoing Practice

This isn't a Ron Popeil rotisserie oven where you can "set it and forget it." Ecosystem alignment takes continuous monitoring. It's like tending a garden. You've got to keep watering it.

That means that you are constantly having to maintain communication throughout the ecosystem. As your ecosystem takes root, consider maintaining communication by doing the following:

- **Monthly ecosystem convenings**—not just to share updates, but to listen, adjust, and align;

- **Shared calendars and visibility tools**—so efforts don't duplicate or collide unintentionally;

- **Cross-sector working groups**—not everyone's a founder, but everyone, including educators, bankers, civic leaders, and broadband providers, has a role;

- **Transparent communication**—share everything, not just the wins and opportunities, but the losses and gaps as well. Silence creates suspicion; openness builds trust.

Check the Ego. Elevate the Mission

You're going to be working with business leaders, elected officials, serial entrepreneurs, and the like. Let's be honest. This work attracts ambitious people. And while that's a good thing, unchecked ambition can fracture ecosystems just as fast as apathy.

You can't build a community-wide initiative if everyone's trying to be the star.

Not every organization will lead every time. That's OK.

This isn't about keeping score. It's about keeping faith in each other and in the mission.

If your organization steps back on one initiative, it should feel like it's passing the baton, not losing ground.

Less Org Chart; More Neural Network

When you think of what you're building, don't picture your ecosystem like a triangle, with a few leaders at the top. Picture it like a neural network with a web of interdependent nodes, each strengthening the system through connection and communication.

In this model, you want your leadership to be distributed. You want the energy to be able to flow where it is needed. And you want the strength of the ecosystem to come from redundancy, not hierarchy. You want everyone in your community sharing your story and talking about why your city is a great place to start a business. That's how real innovation ecosystems behave. Not like rigid trees. Like living, learning systems.

Alignment Is the Glue

When you create a rigid structure, it's brittle. It breaks under pressure. It simply lacks the flexibility to be adaptive. But alignment? Alignment is flexible. It holds under stress.

When your ecosystem sees the same big picture, trusts each other's intent, and stays rooted in shared values, you don't have to worry about the individual tasks, nor do you need to micromanage the process.

When there is alignment, people move in sync because they believe in the same destination.

You just have to make sure that the structure you are building is flexible enough to bend. People and organizations need room to breathe and flexibility to grow. Once your stakeholders are properly aligned, your ecosystem will find its rhythm. And once it does that, it won't need permission to grow. It'll just keep going.

Address Turf Wars Before They Start

We live in a global society fueled by competition. Our businesses are competing for customers with businesses in Asia. Our farmers are competing with produce from Latin America. And our startups are competing for capital with startups in Europe. But in small cities, the ecosystem isn't competing with the rest of the world.

Too often, it's competing with itself.

That's not because people are malicious. It's because resources are tight, identities are tied to institutions, and the pond is only so big. When leaders feel their visibility, funding, or influence is threatened, they dig in. They protect their turf.

But if we want to build a thriving startup ecosystem, we can't afford silos.

Call It Out, Early and Respectfully

When it comes to working with community stakeholders, whether they're university leaders, chamber executives, nonprofit heads, or startup mentors, you are bound to run into people wanting to take credit. City managers want to make sure their city council members are in the spotlight. Nonprofit executive directors want to make sure that their boards are happy. Sharing credit is generally not a problem. But when highlighting the contributions of one group results in alienating another, problems can arise. I like to tell stakeholders, "The choice is simple. We can either compete for credit, or we can collaborate for impact."

Three Ways to Keep Turf Wars in Check

If you're serious about building a culture of collaboration, don't leave it to chance. Build habits and systems that reduce friction before it starts.

1. Clarify Overlapping Missions

One of the most noticeable examples of a disjointed ecosystem is when two groups are running similar programs or, worse, when they are running similar events at the same time. It sends the message that your stakeholders don't communicate and confuses the very people that they profess to help, the entrepreneurs. You don't want your entrepreneurs to feel as though they have to choose between a mentorship cohort and a pitch event; instead, bring them to the table together. Work to align calendars so that activities are spread out throughout the year, giving entrepreneurs the opportunity to engage with your ecosystem all the time, rather than only in a handful of months.

Work to cross-promote programs so that you amplify each other's reach. This could be as simple as an in-kind exchange for marketing where the logos of two entities are placed on each other's marketing material to help extend programs and organizational brands to new audiences.

And when possible, combine efforts to reduce redundancy and increase reach. When you do these things, you're not just saving resources. You're modeling partnership.

2. Celebrate Shared Wins

Too often, we chase headlines and credit like it's the endgame. But in ecosystem work, shared success is the only sustainable success. You need to get into that habit of drawing attention to the collective effort of the ecosystem and to your specific organization. Start using language like:

- "This was a win for the ecosystem."

- "We couldn't have done this without our partners at [org name]."

- "What made this work was the collaboration."

Make it normal, even expected, to shine the spotlight on others. When you celebrate a success grant or open a new entrepreneurship hub, consider substituting the plaque on the building that calls out the names of a few city council members or development authority board members with the names of all the city staff that helped contribute to its success, the university team members that helped write the grant and are delivering the program, and the contractors' employees that helped build the building. Think broadly as to how you share credit. This will help make sure that your effort isn't seen as a "good ole boy" clique and more like a celebration of the many.

3. Incentivize Collaboration

Here's where funders, government agencies, and anchor institutions can really move the needle. Go beyond simply asking for letters of support, and outline meaningful roles and responsibilities that make collaboration a condition of support.

And don't wait for a grant opportunity to start prioritizing collaboration. Look for ways to show cross-sector buy-in and leverage diverse organizations' strengths. This could look something like a university center inviting a local anchor institution to sponsor a reverse pitch competition, where the anchor institution highlights a challenge they face. The program is run in a city facility, and the local SBDC and SCORE team serve as mentors. Each partner promotes the program through their existing network and works with the local news source to amplify the message. You don't need a grant for that. You need collaboration that speaks to the collective vision as well as the individual goals.

Ego Is Expensive

The ecosystem doesn't need more turf wars. They are tiring and undermine all the goodwill you are trying to generate. Focus instead on ways to build trust.

You ought to be asking yourself and your peers:

- Are we more focused on owning programs or advancing outcomes?

- Do we care more about who gets the credit or who gets the opportunity?

Because at the end of the day, no one organization can do it all. And in a small city, everyone's success is connected.

Collaboration Is Culture-Building

Avoiding turf wars isn't just about efficiency. It's about setting the tone for how your ecosystem operates.

If your leaders model trust, coordination, and humility, then your startups will do the same.

But if your stakeholders are fighting over territory, don't be surprised when founders struggle to navigate a fragmented landscape.

So get ahead of it. Set the expectation from the beginning that the work you are doing is too important to do alone.

Keep Score, But Keep It Constructive

Capturing metrics—the right metrics—isn't just about knowing what you did; it's about knowing what you're doing and whether what you're doing is making a difference. Tracking progress helps inform decision-making and helps make sure that our time, energy, and resources are being placed appropriately.

And while capturing data and having useful information are essential, it should be used to monitor and improve, not point fingers and belittle. Because when the latter happens, momentum stops.

Use your data to highlight what's working, to identify what needs to change, and to discover pitfalls and dead ends.

And make the data useful. Don't bury it in binders. Use it in monthly convenings, public dashboards, and strategic planning sessions. Let it fuel curiosity, not conflict.

When you track outcomes and make them visible, you create more opportunities for people to meaningfully engage in the ecosystem conversation. You generate more discussions centered on how many entrepreneurs you are reaching, whether you are reaching the right entrepreneurs, how many businesses you are creating, etc. It's not about trying to reach a certain milestone. It's about enhancing visibility, adaptability, and shared learning.

If the only reason we measure is to point fingers or assign blame, we'll end up with disengaged partners and surface-level wins. But if we measure to learn, align, and improve, then scorekeeping becomes a tool for growth.

What Ecosystem Scorekeeping Looks Like

Let's reframe what success tracking actually means in a living, community-driven startup ecosystem. You're not just counting widgets. You're mapping energy. You're identifying friction points. You're celebrating progress.

A strong ecosystem scorecard might include:

- **Program Participation**
  - Who's showing up?
  - Are the right people being reached (especially underrepresented groups)?
  - What's the retention rate?

- **Startups Launched**
  - How many new ventures came out of local programs or networks?
  - What industries are being represented?

- **Accessed Capital**
  - How much early-stage capital is floating around locally?

- o Are business owners getting the money they need at the right times?

- **Public-Private Partnerships**

  - o Are government entities, colleges, nonprofit organizations, and businesses working together to co-lead initiatives?

  - o Are organizations that used to be siloed now working together?

- **Community Engagement Events**

  - o How often are people gathering around entrepreneurship?

  - o Are new faces participating, or is it the usual suspects?

Don't Forget the Intangibles

Collecting information shouldn't be limited to the things you can easily count. Just because something isn't easy to quantify doesn't mean it's not worth tracking. In fact, it's often the qualitative moments that matter most:

- A high schooler pitching a business idea for the first time;

- A retired entrepreneur offering to mentor a startup;

- A church opening its basement for a weekend pop-up market;

- A banker who never funded startups deciding to take a chance.

These moments are signs of culture shift. And culture shift is the leading indicator of a thriving ecosystem.

If you focus solely on numerical metrics, you're failing to see the bigger picture. While numbers measure growth, the stories sustain progress. Just think about the stories of Bill Gates, Michael Dell, and Mark Zuckerberg. Their stories of dropping out of college and building billion-dollar empires move our hearts and inspire our actions. They not only built powerful brands, but they also inspired countless would-be entrepreneurs to embark on their own entrepreneurial journey.

Progress Over Perfection

Regardless of the size of your city, creating an ecosystem takes time and effort. The goal isn't to check boxes but to build momentum.

So yes, keep score. But do it with grace, with context, and with the understanding that every partner is learning, adapting, and growing right alongside the startups they serve. For when accountability is collaborative, it becomes a powerful force in fueling the growth of your ecosystem.

Leadership Isn't About Control; It's About Stewardship

When it comes to building a startup ecosystem, leadership is not about being in charge. It's about being in service; that's why you're stewards.

Too often, we equate leadership with control. We think of it as making the decisions, owning the mic, getting the credit. But in ecosystem work, ego is the enemy of real progress.

The strongest leaders I've seen in this space aren't the ones with the biggest titles or the longest resumes. They're the ones who know how to create space for others to shine, how to elevate voices that are often overlooked, and how to stay relentlessly focused on long-term outcomes, not short-term recognition.

Stewardship Means Tending, Not Owning

Think of your startup ecosystem as a community garden. You don't force things to grow in your garden. You simply nurture their growth. That's what stewardship is. It's about you watering relationships. Pulling weeds when turf wars pop up. Inviting new hands into the soil. And most importantly, staying patient and giving your crop time to grow.

Your job is to tend, not to control. The ecosystem isn't yours. It belongs to the community. Your role is to guide, to support, and to model the kind of trust and transparency you want the whole network to embody.

What Ecosystem Stewardship Looks Like in Practice

True ecosystem leaders commit to actions that don't always make the headlines.

Listening More Than Talking: When you start campaigning for your ecosystem, people are going to start looking at you for all the answers. Instead of feeling pressure to respond, commit to listening and working together to find the answers. And be present in conversations where you're not the center.

Building Bridges Across Silos: If university students don't know what the small business development center is doing or if the city council isn't hearing from entrepreneurs, your ecosystem is fragmented. Stewards connect the dots.

Championing the Work When No One's Watching: The unsung email intro. The weekend call with a struggling founder. The extra push to get the grant application out the door. These small acts of service create the invisible scaffolding of an ecosystem.

Leadership That Lasts

If your leadership team can stay aligned in vision, humble in execution, and accountable to the community, then you're not just managing a project; you're building a culture. A movement. And five years from now, when that once-skeptical city council member is bragging about the startup that scaled from Main Street, or when a high schooler becomes the next ecosystem success story, you'll realize that you didn't build a brand. You built a legacy.

That's the power of stewardship. That's the kind of leadership small cities need. And that's what will transform your startup ecosystem from a collection of parts into a thriving, connected network.

PART III

BUILDING THE INFRASTRUCTURE

Chapter 5: Developing Entrepreneurial Programs and Spaces

"You don't have to be a genius or visionary or even a college graduate to be successful. You just need a framework and a dream."

-Michael Dell, *founder Dell, Technologies*

By the time you make it to this point, you are probably feeling really good about where you are. And you should. You've brought the right people together and crafted a shared vision. You've also clarified your values and set the direction for where your ecosystem is headed.

You're that much closer to turning the idea of an ecosystem in your city into reality.

But momentum only matters if it's channeled into meaningful, visible action. That means that you must create the conditions for entrepreneurs to actually build.

Offer more than just encouragement or cheerleading. Put in place real tools, real programs, and real places where ideas can become businesses and people with potential can become founders.

This happens through two foundational pillars: programs and spaces.

1. Programs

These are your systems of support that your entrepreneurs need. The educational workshops, accelerator cohorts, pitch nights, mentorship networks, and startup weekends. Programs give structure to the entrepreneurial journey. They help new founders go from "I have an idea" to "I know my next step."

And just as importantly, they send a message about your ecosystem. They say that your community is serious about supporting entrepreneurs.

2. Spaces

These are your physical environments where your entrepreneurs can gather. They are the shared workspaces, coffee shop corners, library innovation labs, or even church fellowship halls used after hours. In ecosystems, spaces aren't just about real estate.

They're about building professional connections and finding collaborators. They are about creating places where people can gather, meet, ideate, and inspire one another.

You don't need glass walls or million-dollar architecture to do this. Instead, you need intentionality. You need to have spaces that are welcoming, affordable, and designed with your local entrepreneurs in mind.

If a startup ecosystem is a living organism, then:

- Programs are its muscles—driving growth, adaptation, and movement;

- Spaces are its bones—offering structure, stability, and a place for things to take root.

You need both. One without the other results in imbalance. They can lead to a bunch of ideas but no momentum, or a bunch of activity but no community.

As you set out to think about your programs and spaces, don't overthink it. This doesn't have to be complicated. Most small cities don't need a 25,000-square-foot innovation hub or a Silicon Valley-style incubator with kombucha taps and nap pods. What they need is a deep understanding of what local entrepreneurs actually need and the will to build with them, not just for them.

That's where this chapter begins. With a shift away from glossy models and toward grounded solutions.

Because when you design programs and spaces in partnership with your community, the dream of entrepreneurship becomes accessible and the ecosystem begins to come alive.

Build Programs That Solve Real Problems

Let's get one thing straight: the goal of an entrepreneurial program is not to fill seats or win grant dollars. It's to move people forward.

In small cities especially, we can't afford to waste time (or trust) on programming that looks good on paper but doesn't actually serve the needs of the people it claims to support. We have to start with asking, "What do our entrepreneurs need most right now, and how can we help them take their next step?"

That might sound simple, but it's where many ecosystems go off course. They start with the solution—a bootcamp, a speaker series, a weekend hackathon—before truly understanding the problem. But good programming isn't just well-funded. It's well-aligned.

It's built around the real, everyday struggles of early-stage founders.

Here's what that usually means:

- **How to validate an idea.**

  Most new founders aren't short on passion. They're short on feedback. They need structured ways to test their assumptions, talk to customers, and avoid spending months building something nobody wants.

- **How to find (and keep) customers.**

  Marketing can feel overwhelming. Founders need help understanding customer discovery, pricing models, channels, and how to create real value that leads to repeat business.

- **How to build a team.**

  No one builds a business alone. Programs should offer guidance on how to recruit talent, delegate, build culture, and avoid burnout. In small cities, this often means tapping into unconventional talent pools. Area students, retirees, or even family members can serve as initial team members.

- **How to pitch for capital.**

  Whether it's a local microloan or an angel round, entrepreneurs need help articulating their value, presenting financials, and understanding what banks and investors look for.

- **How to navigate the basics.**

  Understanding concepts like legal structure, tax obligations, digital marketing, operations, and procurement isn't glamorous, but these are areas where many good ideas die if entrepreneurs don't have access to clear, local guidance.

Founder First: Always

The best programs aren't designed to impress a grant committee; they're designed to serve the founder.

That means:

- Keeping things lean and flexible;

- Making space for trial and error;

- Measuring success by entrepreneur progress, not just attendance or photos for social media.

You don't need a 12-week accelerator out of the gate. You can start with a one-night workshop at the library or a mentorship lunch in the back room of a diner. The key is to start small, test quickly, and listen constantly.

If something works, grow it. If it doesn't, fix it or let it go.

The key is to craft something that is reflective of your community and valued by your entrepreneurs.

Program Mistakes to Avoid

It's easy to blame a lack of funds for the inability to sustain a program. But if we're being honest, most startup ecosystem programs don't fail because of a lack of money. They fail because of a lack of alignment.

Over the years, I've seen well-meaning communities spend thousands—sometimes hundreds of thousands—on flashy initiatives that never gain traction. Not because people didn't care. But because they skipped the basics.

So before you launch another workshop series or pitch competition, hit pause and make sure you're not falling into these common traps:

1. Copy-Pasting Models From Bigger Cities

I can't count how many times I've heard someone say, "Let's just do what Austin did," or "Boulder has this amazing model. Can we just bring that here?"

When you're building an ecosystem, it's tempting to look at other cities, identify key programs, and think that bringing them to your city will give your efforts a needed shot in the arm. After all, we've been conditioned to avoid reinventing the wheel.

But ecosystem building isn't like opening a new franchise. The assets are different. The conditions are different. And the people are different.

That is why you can't just pluck a program from a model city and expect it to work. That's because what works in a dense, venture-rich tech hub won't automatically translate to a rural community with one coffee shop and no Uber coverage. Instead of copying the surface-level features of someone else's success, you need to be committed to doing the work. Understand the conditions that made that success possible and ask whether those conditions exist in your backyard.

Build for your context, not for someone else's headlines.

2. Overdesigning Programs

Another trap to avoid is confusing complexity with quality.

I've seen programs spend months crafting elaborate intake processes, curriculum guides, and branding strategies only to burn out the team and frustrate entrepreneurs before a single session is delivered.

The best programs are simple, human, and responsive. You don't need a 30-slide deck or a three-tiered funnel model. You just need to get people in the room, solve real problems, and create momentum.

Don't fall into paralysis by analysis where you are so concerned about building the perfect program that you fail to launch.

Focus on outcomes, not optics. And remember that done is better than perfect.

3. Measuring Attendance Over Impact

It's easy to fall into the vanity metric game. This is especially true when funders want to see numbers and new supporters want to talk about the number of "likes" or "clicks" a particular post received.

While a packed room looks good in a photo, if no one leaves with new knowledge, a clear next step, or renewed confidence in their idea, then what was the point?

Success isn't a full room; it's a founder moving forward.

Instead of focusing on butts in seats, ask:

- Did someone take their first step toward launching?

- Did they meet a mentor who changed their thinking?

- Did they find the courage to pitch their idea?

Make sure that you're measuring progress at the founder level. If you're not, then you're missing the whole point.

4. Leaving Out Underrepresented Founders

Most people would agree that your community is stronger when it benefits the most people, most of whom see themselves in the entrepreneurial journey.

If your programs aren't intentionally designed to include women, people of color, immigrants, veterans, rural entrepreneurs, and others who've been excluded from traditional startup pipelines, then you're reinforcing the very barriers you claim to be breaking down.

Inclusion doesn't happen by accident. It takes:

- Outreach beyond your usual networks;

- Diverse facilitators and mentors;

- Accessible locations and times;

- Sliding-scale fees or free options;

- Childcare, transportation support, and translation when needed.

If your ecosystem only works for the top 10%, then it's not an ecosystem. It's a club. Be intentional in your pursuit and launch programs that have the broadest reach. Remember, you're changing the narrative. You want as many voices in your community talking about their success in launching a business in your city. Plus, you never know where that next great idea is going to come from.

Keep It Real, Keep It Relevant

At the end of the day, building great programs isn't about impressing funders or mirroring Silicon Valley. It's about meeting your entrepreneurs where they are and walking with them forward.

Avoid these traps, and you'll save yourself time, money, and frustration. More importantly, you'll build something that actually works for the people who matter most. Your founders.

Create Spaces That Reduce Friction and Spark Belonging

When I say that space matters, I don't just mean real estate. I mean place. Environments where people can come together, collide, connect, and build something bigger than themselves.

Physical spaces shape behavior. They send signals. They create context. When done right, they say, "You belong here. Your ideas matter. And you're not building alone."

And in small cities where serendipity doesn't happen on every corner, these spaces aren't just useful. They're catalytic.

That said, you don't need a million-dollar innovation center to get started. You don't need a name-brand architect, exposed brick, or espresso on tap.

What you need is to be purposeful.

Think Culture, Not Construction

A space can be humble and still be transformative. A donated storefront can become a launchpad. A library conference room can host pitch nights. A university classroom after hours can double as a founder bootcamp. I've even seen a local bar become an unofficial HQ for startup meetups. They all worked because the energy was authentic.

It's not about the square footage. It's about the sense of possibility that lives in that space.

When entrepreneurs walk in, do they feel:

- Welcomed?

- Respected?

- Inspired to take the next step?

If the answer is yes, you're on the right track.

Reduce Friction

One of the biggest barriers to entrepreneurship in small cities isn't lack of talent; it's lack of access. Friction kills momentum. If a new founder has to drive 40 minutes, pay for parking, find a sitter, and navigate five layers of bureaucracy just to attend a workshop, they probably won't come back.

Your job is to make showing up easy.

That means:

- Walkable locations (or at least on a bus route);

- Consistent hours and availability;

- Clear signage, open doors, welcoming staff;

- Child-friendly setups or adjacent family zones/child care centers.

The more accessible your space is, the more likely you are to attract entrepreneurs who've historically been left out of the conversation.

Spark Belonging

Launching a business can feel like a risky and lonely endeavor. It doesn't have to feel that way. Creating a space for entrepreneurship to flourish is more about creating a culture of inclusion, collaboration, and shared ownership than about tables and chairs.

The best entrepreneurial spaces feel less institutional and more like home. I don't mean in the literal sense, but in the way they make people feel safe to try, fail, learn, and grow.

That requires:

- Diverse imagery on the walls and in the programming;

- Bilingual signage if your city has a multilingual population;

- Founders leading sessions, not just sitting in them;

- A norm of mutual support, not competition.

If someone walks in and sees no one who looks like them, hears language they don't understand, or feels like an outsider in a members-only club, then they won't stay.

But if they walk in and hear someone say, "Glad you're here. What are you working on?" Then you've already won.

Start With What You Have, Build With Who You Know

You don't need a fancy innovation hub to build community. You just need a place where people feel seen, supported, and surrounded by possibility.

Start with what you've got:

- A spare room;

- A local coffee shop;

- A borrowed space from a community partner.

Don't worry that the space isn't perfect or doesn't capture what you're trying to build. At this stage, the important thing is just to start.

And while it can be exciting to talk about building a new incubator or coworking space, at the end of the day, spaces don't create ecosystems; people do. But the right space can give those people the confidence, connection, and spark they need to launch the future.

Design Spaces That Do More Than Look Good

It's easy to get swept up in the aesthetics. Shiny floors. Sleek furniture. A nameplate that reads "Innovation Center" in brushed steel.

But no entrepreneur ever launched a company because the building they were in had a cool paint job or polished cement floors.

If you're going to invest in a dedicated space like an innovation hub, a coworking site, or a micro-incubator, make sure it earns its keep. That means it's not just beautiful but also useful. It works. It serves. It solves real problems.

And most importantly, it moves people forward.

Too many communities spend big dollars building gorgeous spaces, only to find them empty six months later. Why? Because they treated the space as the solution, not the platform.

Your innovation center should be a living, breathing tool. It should be anchored by programs, powered by relationships, and buzzing with the kind of founder-focused energy that builds momentum day after day.

Things to Keep in Mind

When you get to the point of addressing your physical infrastructure or your space where entrepreneurship will live in the community, keep these three things in mind:

1. Purpose over polish. The space doesn't have to look like a tech campus. It's okay to look like a working office. A place to get things done.

2. Programs over posters. You don't have to depend on murals or motivating phrases. Give your founders a reason to show up by setting up regular training, office hours, and peer sessions.

3. Prioritize people over prestige. Don't wait for big-name VCs or national press. Lean into the talent you already have in your community: retired professionals, local faculty, and the founders themselves.

The Lesson: Don't Overbuild, Activate

Before you pour resources into a 10,000-square-foot facility, ask yourself:

- What will happen here on Monday morning?

- Who will lead programming?

- How will founders benefit from this tangibly, immediately, and consistently?

- Who owns the energy in this place when the ribbon-cutting ends?

A space, no matter how big or small, is only as valuable as the activity it hosts, the connections it facilitates, and the trust it builds.

So yes, if you can build a dedicated space, do it with pride. But build it with purpose. Build it with people. And build it for progress.

Because the real innovation isn't in the architecture, it's in what the community does with it.

Programs + Spaces = Momentum

If you want to see an ecosystem grow, not just launch but truly take off, you have to understand the quiet power of momentum.

Big, one-time events don't start startup ecosystems. They grow through the steady, cumulative value of everyday interactions, chances, and tiny wins that add up over time.

That's where your spaces and programs come in. They make a loop that keeps becoming stronger when they are well planned and connected. Every achievement sets the stage for the next one. Every meeting brings something fresh.

Let me show you how it works in real life:

- A college student goes to a startup bootcamp and learns how to pitch their idea.

- They get an offer for six months of free coworking space after they finish the bootcamp. No strings attached, simply a place to work and feel like you belong.

- One afternoon, they sit next to a local business owner who is working hard to start their own firm. A simple chat develops into an introduction to finance.

- That relationship leads to a successful pitch for a microgrant that gives them enough money to make a prototype and test it.

- A few months later, that same founder is giving a speech at an entrepreneurial event over coffee, encouraging two

> more people who felt "this world wasn't for people like me."

And on it goes.

The Power Is in the Loop

This isn't just a feel-good story; it's the blueprint. Programs introduce knowledge. Spaces enable connection. Together, they generate opportunity.

And more importantly, they make success visible.

That visibility matters. It fuels belief. It invites participation. It whispers to the next dreamer, "There's a place for you here."

When people see others from their school, their neighborhood, or their background creating something real, they begin to imagine that they could too.

That's momentum. And you don't get there by accident.

Don't Think Sprint—Think Cycle

Too often, communities approach ecosystem building like a sprint. "Let's launch a new program by the end of the quarter." "Let's cut the ribbon on our new space before the next board meeting."

But ecosystems aren't corporate projects. They're organic systems of trust, action, and reinforcement.

Remember, what you're building is more like a flywheel than a finish line. Every founder who finds support, every mentor who gives their time, and every student who attends a demo day is a turn of the wheel. And over time, the movement becomes its own magnet.

The Takeaway

Make sure you get the programs right when you're developing the infrastructure. Make them thin, quick, and focused on the founder.

Make sure to plan spaces with a purpose. Make them easy to get to, welcoming, and full of activity.

But more than anything, connect the dots.

Build the systems where a workshop leads to a relationship, where an unscheduled meeting in the breakroom turns into a deal, and where one founder's win becomes the next founder's start.

That's how ecosystems grow.

Not through heroic efforts.

But through cycles of shared value.

And once that cycle starts spinning, it's hard to stop.

Action Checklist: Getting Started with Programs and Spaces

So you've got the vision. You've gathered your leadership team. You're ready to take action. Now comes the roll-up-your-sleeves part. You will be building the programming and physical anchors that will bring your ecosystem to life.

This isn't about throwing money at the wall or launching a dozen initiatives at once and seeing what sticks. It's about being community-informed, strategic, and focused. Here are a few tips as to how to get started:

1. Survey Local Entrepreneurs About Their Biggest Challenges

Before you plan a single workshop or rent a single building, talk to your entrepreneurs. Not just the polished founders that are accustomed to pitching on stage. Talk to the side-hustlers, the kitchen-table business builders, and the students with big ideas.

Ask them:

- What's holding you back?

- Where do you need help?

- What kind of support would actually move the needle?

This is your grounding point. If your programming doesn't reflect lived experience, it's just noise.

2. Map Existing Training, Coworking, and Mentoring Assets

When it comes to identifying entrepreneurial programs, you probably have more than you think.

Look for:

- Local workforce programs that could be adapted for startups;

- University classrooms that sit empty after hours;

- Retired executives willing to mentor;

- Business competitions or pitch events that already exist, even if informal.

The key is to name it, connect it, and align it. Ecosystems grow when assets are coordinated, not duplicated.

3. Start With a Single Pilot Program Then Test and Learn

Resist the urge to do everything at once.

Pick one real problem, design a lean program to address it, and treat it like a startup itself.

Test. Gather feedback. Iterate.

Maybe it's a 4-week idea validation bootcamp.

Maybe it's a monthly lunch-and-learn led by local founders.

Whatever it is, start small and stay flexible.

4. Identify at Least One "Home Base" for Startup Activity

Find a spot to start. A physical place, however humble, where energy can concentrate.

This doesn't have to be a dedicated space specific to entrepreneurs. It could be:

- A library conference room on Tuesday nights;

- A shared office with rotating entrepreneur residencies;

- A donated space from a civic partner or downtown landlord.

Place creates presence. When people can gather, meet, and feel seen, the ecosystem starts to feel real.

5. Build Cross-Sector Partnerships to Lower Cost and Boost Legitimacy

Remember that you're building community. So, don't go it alone.

Invite a wide cross section of organizations to the table:

- Universities to lend faculty, to encourage student participation, or to make space available;

- Banks to host workshops or to provide microgrants;

- Chambers and EDOs to amplify your events and encourage their members to participate;

- Nonprofits to co-host and co-design inclusive programming.

Collaboration stretches your capacity and widens your reach. It also signals to the community that this isn't a pet project of a small group, but a shared priority.

6. Track Outcomes, Not Just Participation

Sure, it's nice when you fill a room for an event. But that's not impact.

Look deeper at your metrics and measure:

- How many founders launched something new;

- How many got connected to funding, mentors, or customers;

- How confidence or clarity improved after your program.

Don't just count heads and likes; count progress. And use that data to refine, refocus, and grow.

7. Share Success Stories Early and Often

Momentum is fueled by storytelling.
Highlight:

- The mompreneur who landed her first paying customer;

- The college student who pitched for the first time;

- The side-hustler who found a collaborator at your meetup.

Share these stories online, at city council meetings, in university newsletters, and on social media platforms with a common tag.

Make entrepreneurship visible and relatable.

Because when people see that others like them are doing it, they start to believe they can too.

Start Where You Are; Build With What You Have

Every thriving ecosystem you admire started somewhere—with a few committed people, a handful of partners, and a clear intention.

Programs and spaces don't need to be perfect. They just need to be purposeful.

And when they are, they become more than resources.

They become the heartbeat of your local startup movement.

Serve First, Scale Second

One thing I've come to appreciate is that founders don't need more fanfare. They just need more focus. Not on buzzwords or big-dollar infrastructure. But on real, hands-on support that meets them where they are.

And yet, time and again, I've seen ecosystems get built backward. Designed in conference rooms instead of coffee shops. Planned by well-meaning professionals who've never had to max out a credit card to make payroll or cold-call their first customer. It's not that they don't care. It's that they're not close enough to the ground to see what really matters.

Don't make that mistake.

Start with your entrepreneurs. Ask them what they need. Then listen like you mean it. Then build like it matters.

Because when you adopt a serve-first philosophy, you build trust. And when trust grows, the energy in your ecosystem starts to flow. And when energy flows, good things start to scale in a way that is natural, sustainable, and authentic.

You don't need to start with a million-dollar incubator, and you don't need to be able to answer every question that comes your way.

You just need to show up consistently, humbly, and in service of the people doing the work.

Don't make it too hard on yourself or overly complicated. Start with:

- A single program that helps someone turn a side hustle into a first invoice;

- A simple space where founders can find community and conversation;

- A standing meeting where local leaders listen to what's working and what's missing.

That's where ecosystems begin.

Not in policy memos. Not in press releases.

But in quiet rooms, when someone dares to share an idea and someone else leans in and says, "Let's build around that."

So here's your charge:

- Serve first.

- Build trust.

- Let scale be the byproduct, not the goal.

Because when your ecosystem becomes recognized as a place that genuinely supports its builders, more builders will come. And when they do, they won't just create companies; they'll create culture, momentum, and a shared sense of purpose that no outside playbook can replicate.

That's how small cities build big futures.

CHAPTER 6:
ATTRACTING
AND SUPPORTING
ENTREPRENEURS

"You can dream, create, design and build the most wonderful place in the world...but it requires people to make it a reality."

-Walt Disney, *co-founder, The Walt Disney Company*

Depending on your age, when you hear the phrase, "If you build it, he will come," you may conjure an image of Kevin Costner's character, Ray Kinsella, walking through a cornfield in the movie *Field of Dreams*.

The phrase has been adopted and overused in business as a way of conveying that if you build something of quality, something that evokes emotion, people will buy it.

It's a catchy line from a great film.

But you're not making a movie.

You're building something that can't be scripted into reality—no matter how much care you put into it or how much quality goes into the construction.

Just building a coworking space, launching a startup competition, or rolling out a flashy new program doesn't guarantee entrepreneurs will show up. And even when they do, showing up once doesn't mean they'll stay.

Why? Because founders go where the conditions are right. Where the soil is healthy. Where they feel supported, connected, and seen. And in many small and mid-sized communities, those conditions haven't existed in a long time, or if they have, they haven't been visible or accessible to those outside a select few networks.

Too often, we think the infrastructure will do the heavy lifting for us.

We launch a space and wait.

We host a hackathon and hope.

We assume that momentum can be reverse-engineered through events and signage.

But attraction doesn't work that way.

You don't earn trust or talent by hanging a sign. You earn it by doing the work. Consistently. Quietly. Relationally.

This chapter is about how to earn that trust.

How to shift the perception of your city from "a place people leave" to "a place people build in."

How to support the entrepreneurs already in your midst, especially the ones who've never thought of themselves as "startups," and how to signal to others that this is a place where innovation isn't just possible … it's happening.

We'll cover:

- What makes a city attractive to early-stage founders;

- How to create a reputation for responsiveness, not just resources;

- Why storytelling and relationship-building matter more than branding;

- And what it takes to retain the builders you already have before chasing ones you don't.

We'll focus on the intangible qualities because most communities already have the raw materials. The assets.

What's missing isn't potential. It's visibility, coordination, and consistent support.

If you want entrepreneurs to come, and more importantly, to stay, you have to create a city worth building in not just visiting. That takes time, trust, and follow-through.

And it starts right here.

Start With Who's Already Here

Before you print the brochures, book the keynote speakers, or chase down tech founders from out of state, pause and look around.

Because more often than not, the entrepreneurial seeds you're looking for have already been planted. They're right there, growing quietly in the cracks of your community. And they're doing it without a roadmap, without resources, and often without recognition.

Get to Know Adam – Real World Example

When I talk about building an entrepreneurial ecosystem, I'm not talking about abstract theories or PowerPoint models. I'm talking about people. People whose actions, values, and vision shape the culture of a place so profoundly that you can feel their influence in every corner of the community. For the residents in Statesboro, Georgia, one of those people is Adam.

Most people in the community know Adam from his family restaurants. But if you stop there, you miss the bigger story. In addition to the restaurants, Adam is a master storyteller.

I remember sitting with Adam one afternoon when he described his early days, working insane hours to get one of his ventures off the ground. But even then, Adam was thinking about how to help other entrepreneurs. He was already talking to students about entrepreneurship and showing them that building something of value is about more than profit margins.

One day, while working in the incubator, he met Jim. Jim was a recent college graduate, and he loved to tinker. He would work in the makerspace and could weld, cut, or forge just about anything. On this particular day, Jim had just finished a wooden tumbler crafted from the same white oak as a whiskey barrel. The outside was stained a rich brown color, and the inside was charred black.

Always searching for new ideas and bold thinkers, Adam struck up a conversation with Jim. He wanted to know his story. His passion.

The two fed off each other's energy, and it wasn't too long before they joined forces to launch Whiskey Grail, a company that manufactures handcrafted wooden tumblers designed to enhance the drinking experience of whiskey, bourbon, or rum.

In just its first two years of operations, Whiskey Grail grew from a concept to selling more than 400 tumblers per week! And Jim is only one of many who have benefited from Adam's collaborative spirit. Each month, Adam interacts with five to ten entrepreneurs looking to start or expand their business.

What makes Adam indispensable to the ecosystem isn't just his success. It's how he treats success. He views it as a shared resource. He's the first to show up at a fundraiser, the first to ask if there's anything he can do to help, and the first to tell a young founder, "You can do this, and here's how."

He's also a powerful storyteller. He runs a PR firm, a marketing firm, and a local podcast that highlights local entrepreneurs and community leaders. In a small city like Statesboro, that matters. The ecosystem isn't built on billion-dollar exits or tech unicorns; it's built on trust, collaboration, and leaders who know that we rise or fall together. Adam embodies that truth. He proves, day after day, that you can be ambitious and community-minded at the same time. That you can scale your dreams without shrinking your generosity.

When I look at the future of Statesboro's entrepreneurial ecosystem, I see Adam's fingerprints all over it. Not because he set out to be the "face" of anything, but because he lives the values that make a community thrive. In an age where so many are chasing the next big thing, Adam's greatest contribution might be reminding us that the most enduring success is the kind you build together.

Your first job isn't to attract. It's to acknowledge the contributions of people like Adam. The ones that already embody the entrepreneurial spirit of your ecosystem.

When it comes to identifying them, I want you to ask yourself:

- Who's building websites from the back booth of a coffee shop?

- Who's been crafting candles, printing shirts, or repairing bikes in their garage?

- Who started a catering business during the pandemic but never got beyond Facebook posts?

- Which high school students are flipping sneakers or selling handmade jewelry on Etsy?

- Where are the informal meetups happening? It doesn't matter if these are techies at the brewery, creatives at the library, or freelancers swapping stories over coffee.

These aren't "potential entrepreneurs." They are entrepreneurs. They just haven't been invited into the ecosystem—yet.

And here's the mistake I see all too often. Some cities get enamored with importing founders instead of investing in the ones they already have. They chase outside validation by offering relocation bonuses or contracting with out-of-state startup accelerators before cultivating internal resilience.

But if you ignore your own talent, you build an ecosystem on shaky ground. It's like constructing a house while pretending the existing foundation doesn't matter.

Instead, I want you to do the following:

- **Go local.** Host listening sessions with homegrown founders.

- **Be present.** Show up to pop-up markets, student showcases, and business mixers. Go to listen, not to speak.

- **Build trust.** Offer office hours at coworking spaces or community centers where people already gather.

- **Signal belonging.** Use plain language, diverse imagery, and approachable programming so no one feels entrepreneurship is "only for tech bros with seed funding."

Because there's already an Adam or two in your community. They've been here. Some have tried and stumbled. Others are still grinding quietly. All of them carry insights about what's broken, what's missing, and what's possible.

Before you build a platform, earn their presence. Before you write your pitch deck, find your Adams and understand their pain points.

Don't let your ecosystem be built on assumptions or abstractions. Start with the people. Build from there.

That's how you create a community that doesn't just attract entrepreneurs; it retains them, respects them, and rewards their courage.

Because the best place to find your next startup success story isn't in someone else's city.

It's in your own backyard.

Make Your Ecosystem Navigable

Imagine if someone in your city has an idea. Maybe it's for a mobile app, a food truck, a home-based business, or a new kind of service no one's thought of yet. They're excited. Motivated. Ready to take the first step.

Now ask yourself, do they know where to go?

If your answer starts with, "Well, it depends …"

You've already lost them.

Because the moment someone feels lost, overwhelmed, or invisible, you've created friction. And friction kills momentum.

Too often, we assume entrepreneurs will "figure it out" if they're serious. But that's not how ecosystems work. Thriving startup cities don't rely on scavenger hunts or secret handshakes. They lower the barrier to entry. They make support obvious, visible, and human.

Your job is to ensure that the path from idea to action is clear and feels welcoming, not convoluted.

And don't think you need a lot of resources either. Here are a few things you can do to get the ball rolling without a million-dollar investment or a bureaucracy of gatekeepers:

- **Create a one-stop startup webpage.** It doesn't need bells and whistles. Just a simple, up-to-date page that lists available resources: funding sources, coworking spaces, local mentors, upcoming events, and who to contact. One page. One link. Share it everywhere.

- **Design a visual ecosystem map.** Whether it's a slick graphic or a community bulletin board at the library, make it easy for people to see the connections. Who runs the incubator? What does the chamber offer? Where can you take a basic business class? Show it all in one place.

- **Host a "Startup 101" orientation.** You'll need to figure out the cadence, but it doesn't have to be overwhelming; it just needs to happen. It could be every quarter or even just twice a year. This should be a free, no-pressure info session for first-time founders. Partner with a local college or coffee shop. Keep it casual. The goal is to demystify the process and connect people to people.

- **Designate an ecosystem concierge.** This could be a staff member at a nonprofit, someone at the SBDC, or a rotating role shared by partners. The key is that there's a name and face people can reach out to when they don't know where to start.

Keep in mind that entrepreneurs are often walking into this world with more questions than answers. They're not experts in navigating bureaucracy or piecing together siloed programs.

They need a welcome mat, not a maze.

Because when someone asks, "How do I start a business here?" the answer shouldn't be, "Well, it depends."

It should be, "I'm so glad you asked, and here's where to begin."

That's when you'll know that your ecosystem gets it. It's when the process becomes navigable. By clarifying where to go and who to talk to, you stop losing talent to confusion, and you start building momentum from clarity.

That's when people with Adam-sized ambition stay. And their ideas begin to take shape.

It's not because you had the most resources; it's because you made them accessible.

Build Programs That Match Different Entrepreneur Types

One of the biggest mistakes I see in ecosystem building is the one-size-fits-all approach to program design.

A city launches a bootcamp or hosts a pitch night and expects it to serve everyone. From the college student coding a fintech app, to the mom launching a home bakery, to the retired veteran starting a small landscaping business.

But not all entrepreneurs are the same. And treating them like they are doesn't just miss the mark, it risks alienating the very people you're trying to support.

A strong ecosystem starts with respect. Respect for different dreams. Different definitions of success. Different paces and paths.

When it comes to accessing why, know that different people have different motivations for launching a business:

- Some founders want to build the next big thing and raise venture capital.

- Some want to earn a stable income doing what they love without a boss.

- Some are solving a problem in their neighborhood.

- Some are just trying to create generational wealth for their family.

They all matter. And your programs should reflect that.

So What Does This Look Like in Practice?

- **For high-growth tech founders:** You could offer access to startup accelerators, pitch competitions, and investment readiness bootcamps. Connect them with mentors who've successfully raised capital or scaled companies. Nothing is as powerful as connecting with someone that's been there and done that.

- **For solo entrepreneurs and service-based founders:** You could hold hands-on seminars on how to set prices, manage time, market on a tight budget, and choose the best business structure for their needs. Put customer generation and a simple business model first.

- **For makers and artists:** You might put them in touch with local markets, arts councils, or groups that are all about Etsy. Help them figure out how to do e-commerce, branding, and licensing.

- **For enterprises on Main Street:** You might help them with things like renting a storefront, getting permits in their area, filing taxes, recruiting part-time workers, and getting small business financing.

- **For founders who aren't well represented:** You could offer programming led by people who have been through similar things and that addresses problems such as not being able to get funding, not having enough representation, or not trusting institutions.

Think of your programming as a set of tools. Not everyone needs a drill. Some people only require a wrench and a steady hand.

That means your job isn't just to offer more programs. It's to offer the right programs.

And to get that right, start by listening.

Don't be afraid of customer discovery. Ask real entrepreneurs what they need. Don't just focus on the loudest voices. Reach out to the quiet builders too. Survey them. Host listening sessions. Show up where they already are.

Because when someone walks into your ecosystem and sees a program designed for them—a program that reflects their goals, their stage, and their style; it sends the message that we see you. And you belong here. That's powerful.

That's how you move from programming that checks a box to programming that unlocks potential.

And that's how your city earns a reputation as a great place to start a business. Not just as a place that talks about entrepreneurship, but as one that truly supports all of its entrepreneurs.

Table: Entrepreneur Needs Assessment and Sample Support

Type of Entrepreneur	Needs	Sample Support
First-time founders	Basics of business, peer learning	Bootcamps, cohort-based learning
Underserved entrepreneurs	Trust, access, affordability	Culturally relevant programming, microgrants

Technical founders	Mentors, product-market fit support	Startup accelerators, angel pitch nights
Lifestyle entrepreneurs	Local visibility, easy setup	Marketing workshops, licensing navigation
Youth/Students	Confidence, experimentation space	Innovation labs, hackathons, pitch clubs

The more intentional and focused your programming for entrepreneurs is, the more likely you are to reach and retain a wide variety of builders.

Create Visibility Through Storytelling

Storytelling in ecosystem building is a powerful tool. We'll spend more time focusing on its importance in Chapter 11, but I think it's worth highlighting its importance in attracting new founders to your ecosystem. If you want people to believe that entrepreneurship is possible in your city, they have to see it happening.

Not in theory. Not in five years. Right now.

Too often, small cities pour resources into programs and spaces but forget to tell the stories of the people using them. And without those stories, the broader community, especially would-be founders, never sees the momentum that's building right under their noses.

People can't aspire to what they can't see. And they certainly won't join an ecosystem they don't know exists.

Storytelling is your signal. It tells residents, students, investors, and outsiders:

Something is happening here. People are building. Ideas are becoming real.

And it works both ways. When you tell the story of a local founder who bootstrapped their way to a product launch, you're not just promoting them; you're reinforcing a narrative that this is a city where startups are supported.

So How Do You Make Entrepreneurship Visible?

Here are a few things that you should be doing to help spread the word and inspire the next wave of entrepreneurs:

- **Founder spotlights:** Interview local entrepreneurs and publish their stories in newsletters, newspapers, blogs, or social media. Ask about their "why," their hurdles, and their hopes.

- **Startup success reels:** Capture short videos from demo days, launch events, or mentorship meetups. Share them widely. Use real faces, real energy, and real outcomes.

- **Behind-the-scenes features:** Take people inside the spaces and moments that make the ecosystem work. Don't think everything needs to be polished. It just needs to be authentic. Feature a late-night brainstorm at a coworking hub or a quiet win during office hours.

- **Local media partnerships:** Encourage news outlets to cover startups the way they cover ribbon-cuttings or high school football. As we'll discuss later in the book, entrepreneurship is economic development. It deserves the spotlight.

- **Celebrate the small wins:** A first sale. A new hire. A founder's first time pitching. These may not make national headlines, but locally, they signal progress. And progress attracts more builders.

> **Bonus Tip: Make Storytelling a Shared Responsibility**
>
> Your ecosystem shouldn't rely on one person to capture every win. Empower your partners, the universities, chambers, nonprofits, and your Adams themselves to share stories using common hashtags, shared branding, or collaborative platforms.

The goal isn't perfection. It's presence. A steady drumbeat of visibility that says:

- This city backs its builders.

- You don't have to leave to launch.

- If they can do it, so can you.

Over time, this builds more than awareness; it builds belief that your community is a viable place to start something meaningful.

And belief, more than any grant or facility, is what turns potential into motion.

Attracting External Entrepreneurs: What Actually Works

Once your local foundation is strong, your programs are humming, your founders feel seen, and your leadership is aligned, you'll probably start hearing the question:

"How do we bring more entrepreneurs in?"

It's a fair question. Growth requires new energy. And small cities often benefit when new voices, perspectives, and ideas join the mix.

Somewhere along the way, someone says, "We need to brand ourselves and create a catchy tagline to enhance the visibility of our community."

But entrepreneurs don't move because of a slogan. They move because of value. And they stay because of belonging.

I've seen too many communities spend money on slick ad campaigns positioning themselves as "The Next Silicon Valley" or "America's Hidden Startup Gem" without ever asking what a founder actually needs to thrive.

If you want to attract builders, stop marketing to their ego. Start speaking to their operating reality.

So, What Actually Makes Someone Move?

Entrepreneurs relocate for a combination of:

- **Access to capital or customers:** If your city offers strategic proximity to buyers, suppliers, or early-stage funding, that's a magnet.

- **Quality of life:** Affordability, safety, good schools, outdoor recreation, and livability all matter—especially for entrepreneurs with families.

- **Community and connection:** Founders want to be plugged in, not isolated. They look for mentorship, collaboration, and a feeling of being part of something bigger.

- **Talent pool:** Having a university nearby, or a strong skilled workforce, signals that a founder can build a team, not just a product.

It's not enough to say, "We're a great place to live." You have to say, "We're a great place to build."

The Secret? Own Your Niche

Instead of trying to compete with every other city on every front, focus on where you have a unique advantage. Start by asking:

- What industries are rooted here?

- What stories can we tell that no one else can?

- Who's already thriving in our ecosystem and why?

Then build messaging and experiences around authentic alignment.

Let's take a look at some key initiatives happening in small cities across the Southeastern U.S.

Chattanooga

Chattanooga is often pointed to as one of the first proof points that a mid-sized city can compete on a global stage when it comes to innovation. In 2008, the Electric Power Board (EPB) took a bold step, tapping the bond markets to fund what at the time seemed almost futuristic—a city-wide smart grid and fiber-optic communications network. That investment, coupled with more than \$100 million in federal recovery funds, gave Chattanooga something no one else in the country had: one of the most advanced, municipally owned broadband networks in the world.

That "Gig City" identity became the spark. Instead of simply celebrating faster internet, civic leaders asked a bigger question: how could this infrastructure transform the local economy? Under Mayor Andy Berke's leadership, the city convened stakeholders from across the community, which led to the formation of The Enterprise Center and the launch of Chattanooga's Innovation District in 2015. Anchored by the Edney Innovation Center, EPB, the Lamp Post Group, and the University of Tennessee Chattanooga, the district provided both the physical space and the collaborative framework that allowed startups and entrepreneurs to thrive. Chattanooga showed the rest of us that innovation districts are not just for global megacities—they can be born in smaller, scrappier communities if the right assets are leveraged.

Charleston

Charleston's approach looked very different. In 2001, community leaders in Charleston launched the Charleston Digital Corridor, a nonprofit entity created to promote the city's knowledge economy. It was a city-led effort with little initial university involvement. For a long time, the belief that if you built a supportive environment for tech entrepreneurs, growth would follow fueled it. And it did. Tech jobs grew, wages climbed, and the city began to diversify beyond its traditional reliance on tourism and hospitality.

But Charleston's path also highlights a challenge. Without strong cooperation between universities, private businesses, and the city, efforts tended to be less focused, with innovation happening in many different places. Charleston has only recently started to put together a more unified plan, thanks to new developments like the South Carolina Research Authority (SCRA), the Medical University of South Carolina (MUSC) and the City of Charleston's SCRA MUSC Innovation Center, where an abandoned mattress factory was transformed to include wet labs to attract startups in the biomedical space. It reminds us that while grassroots and city-led projects can get things moving, long-term success frequently depends on working together across sectors.

Greenville, SC

Greenville's story is one of adaptation and persistence. In 2007, local entrepreneurs, city officials, and the Chamber of Commerce came together to launch NEXT Innovation Center, a hub for growing startups in a repurposed downtown space. What's interesting about Greenville is how its leaders weren't afraid to borrow ideas. After seeing what Charleston was building with its Digital Corridor, they retooled their model to better fit Greenville's assets and culture. The result was a triple-helix collaboration—university, government, and private sector—working in tandem. It demonstrated the value of looking beyond one's borders, taking inspiration from peer cities, and tailoring best practices to local conditions.

Augusta, GA

In Augusta, the turning point came from outside the community. When the Department of Defense poured billions into Fort Gordon, the city recognized an opportunity to align its future with national security and cyber innovation. Augusta University, working with the State of Georgia, seized the moment and created the Georgia Cyber Center on the banks of the Savannah River. Opened in 2018 with $100 million in state funding, the center has become a magnet for talent, startups, and federal partners working at the intersection of cybersecurity, defense, and emerging technologies like drones. Augusta exemplifies the potency of harmonizing local strategy with federal investment, enabling smaller communities to capitalize on national priorities while modifying them for their own advantages.

None of these places tried to be everything. But they tried to be something. And they sought to do it well.

Welcoming Outsiders

If your city is already nurturing its local founders, tracking results, and sharing stories with pride, it becomes much easier to invite others in.

When outsiders see a place that supports builders, showcases innovation, and fosters a genuine community, they don't just become curious. They start to ask, "Why not here?"

And when they do, your job is simply to show them they belong.

IBut showing them is more than just talking about it. Patting someone on the back and telling them that their idea is worth pursuing is easy. After all, it's not your money that you're investing. It's not your late nights that you're sacrificing. You're not forgoing the next career step or resume-building project.

After all, if someone is brave enough to try, shouldn't you be bold enough to back them?

But founders don't just need applause. They need tools.

Every city can put on a panel, host a networking night, or issue a press release saying they support entrepreneurship. But if you stop there, you're offering cheerleading, not scaffolding.

You need to be building infrastructure. A support system that makes building in your city possible.

And not a theoretical system. A practical, actionable, ready-to-use list of resources that meet them where they are: in the messy, exhausting middle of trying to build something from nothing.

Here are a few things that you can be doing to help reduce friction and get your entrepreneurs some much-needed traction.

Microgrants for MVP Testing

Start with microgrants in the $500–$2,500 range to help early-stage founders:

- Build a prototype;
- Run ads to test demand;
- Hire a freelance designer;
- Cover legal filing fees.

It's not about the size of the check. While that will help, it's more about the signal that you're sending to the entrepreneur. This shows that we believe in you enough to invest, even at the beginning. And that belief matters more than most people realize.

Expert Office Hours (That Don't Suck)

Bring in subject matter experts that founders need. Bring lawyers, accountants, marketers, and HR professionals in for structured office hours.

But don't just hope people show up. Promote it. Make it founder-friendly:

- Offer 20–30 minute slots (short, focused, efficient);

- Schedule during lunch or early evening;

- Hold them in familiar spaces like coworking hubs, libraries, even breweries;

- Promote the sessions through founder groups and personal outreach.

One conversation with a good CPA or IP attorney can save a founder thousands of dollars and months of headaches.

Founder-Friendly Resource Libraries

Stop making entrepreneurs reinvent the wheel.

Give them a toolkit with templates they can adapt, including:

- Pitch decks with example slides;

- Simple business plan frameworks;

- Sample cap tables and equity calculators;

- Brand kits and media outreach guides;

- Grant and loan application checklists.

Better yet, customize them to your city's reality. Add a local startup guide with:

- Business license info;

- Permit processes;

- Links to city, chamber, and nonprofit programs;

- Local service providers who offer founder-friendly pricing.

Make it easy to move from idea to action. But do so with consideration for the founder.

As you establish programs, identify activities, and pull resources, be sure to respect the founders' time and money. Time and money are the two currencies that matter most to early-stage founders.

So ask yourself:

- Are we wasting either?

- Are we asking people to attend events that don't create value?

- Are we referring them to programs they don't qualify for or don't need yet?

- Are we sending them to five different websites instead of one central resource?

The goal isn't to coddle founders. It's to remove friction.

Make the path smoother. Shorten the distance between confusion and clarity. Between dreaming and doing.

The credibility of your ecosystem is built on how useful it is. If you say you support entrepreneurs but can't show up with tools when it counts, your words will ring hollow.

But if you show up with real, relevant, founder-first resources, especially when no one's watching, you earn trust. And trust is the soil where startups grow.

Avoid These Pitfalls

Building a startup ecosystem is hard work. Sustaining one is even harder. And in that effort, good intentions aren't enough.

Too many cities sabotage their momentum not through malice but through missteps. Well-meaning leaders launch programs, open buildings, or cut ribbons but still see flatlined engagement or frustrated founders.

Why?

Because ecosystems don't thrive on optics or checklists. They thrive on trust, inclusivity, and usefulness.

Here are four common pitfalls I've seen and how to sidestep them.

1. One-Size-Fits-All Programming

It's tempting to design a single program and call it your ecosystem solution. It's efficient, easy to manage, and looks tidy on a slide deck.

But ecosystems aren't homogenous, and your programs shouldn't be either.

The needs of a solo web designer differ from those of a biotech founder. A recent college grad launching a podcast requires different support than a mid-career woman opening a home-based bakery.

When you design with only one archetype in mind (typically white, male, tech-focused, and well-networked), you unintentionally exclude the rest.

A few ways around this are to:

- Offer multiple on-ramps. Allow founders to enter at various stages, based on their individual backgrounds and individual needs.

- Design modular, adaptable programming. You're not designing a college curriculum. Create self-contained units that enable the founder to get the information they need when they need it.

- Engage directly with underrepresented entrepreneurs and co-create with them. Entrepreneurs are more likely to engage in the programming if they had a hand in designing it.

Start with relevance, not reach. People show up for what speaks to them.

2. Over-Reliance on a Single Startup or Founder

Every ecosystem has its Adam. A success story that you're really proud of. And it's tempting to pin your hopes (and press releases) on one shining example.

But what happens if that founder burns out? Moves away? Or their startup fails, as most eventually do?

Ecosystems are powered by people, but they're built on networks.

Highlighting a standout is fine but not at the expense of nurturing others. If one person becomes the face of everything, others may feel like they don't belong.

As you're telling your story, make sure to:

- Celebrate a range of founders, industries, and stages.

- Show that there's room for the early-stage builder, the microbusiness owner, and the seasoned scale-up.

- Tell as many stories as you can. Don't just focus on the loudest one.

Diversification isn't just a good investment strategy; it's a good ecosystem building strategy as well.

3. Unclear Messaging

Imagine you're a new founder in town. You've got an idea, some grit, and a laptop. You Google "[your city] + startup support." What do you find?

If the process requires more than two clicks, or if you find yourself navigating between organizations with unclear missions, you've already lost them.

Confusion kills energy. And when messaging is muddled, momentum dies quietly.

A way to help avoid confusion is to:

- Create a centralized startup portal with clear steps and local contacts.

- Use plain language, not bureaucratic jargon.

- Make it obvious who you help, how you help, and where to go next.

If people don't know where to plug in, they won't.

4. Gatekeeping by Insiders

This is the fastest way to destroy trust.

I've said this before, but I think it's worth repeating. If getting access to mentors, funding, or visibility in your ecosystem depends on knowing the right people or being part of the "in" crowd, then you're not running a startup community. You're running a private club.

And when that happens, you leave out a lot of powerful voices. A lot of opportunities to instill real change in your city. You often leave out women. People of color. First-time founders. Immigrants. Students. Veterans. Anyone who didn't come up through the usual channels.

Gatekeeping doesn't just slow your ecosystem down. It warps its DNA.

While you can't eliminate this from happening—after all, people like to hang around those that they identify with—you can mitigate it by being intentional. Make sure to:

- Publish open application processes for programs and funding.

- Rotate speaking slots and leadership opportunities.

- Track diversity across events and initiatives and be honest about any gaps.

- Train gatekeepers (often unintentionally exclusive) to become door-openers.

Ecosystems grow when new people can walk in and see a place for themselves.

Inclusivity Isn't a Buzzword—It's a Strategy

Strong ecosystems aren't built by accident. They're built by design. They're built through a series of intentional decisions that widen the circle, clarify the path, and support every founder like they matter.

And if you can avoid these common missteps while listening closely to your community, you'll move from programs and promises to real progress.

Action Checklist: Attracting and Supporting Founders

If you want to grow your startup ecosystem, you need to do more than open the doors. You have to invite people in, show them around, and help them feel like they belong. That means making it easy to get started, clear to navigate, and worthwhile to stay.

To help you in your journey, here's a practical, founder-first checklist to guide your next steps:

Map and Engage Existing Founders in Your City

We've established that entrepreneurs are everywhere. Chances are they're already in your community and already doing some amazing things. You just haven't met them yet.

Start by identifying:

- Side hustlers selling online;

- Local service providers (designers, consultants, caterers);

- High schoolers or college students building apps;

- Entrepreneurs who launched quietly during the pandemic.

Use high school counselors, college deans, church pastors, and online platforms like LinkedIn, Upwork, TikTok, and Facebook to identify them. But once you've found them. Invite them to the table and give them a voice.

> **Bonus Tip:** Host a "Founders You Should Know" networking lunch. You'll be surprised who shows up and who brings a friend.

Create a Clear, Visible Entry Point for Startup Support

Making things clear online is one thing, but if a first-time founder has to ask five people before finding the right resource, you've got a visibility problem.

Try to make things as simple for the new entrepreneur as possible. Start by doing the following:

- A dedicated "Start Here" webpage for entrepreneurs;

- A single point of contact or ecosystem coordinator;

- An easy-to-navigate visual map of who does what.

Think of it as an on-ramp to the highway. The smoother it is, the more people merge in.

Segment Your Support Programming by Founder Type

Not every entrepreneur is chasing a billion-dollar valuation, and they shouldn't have to in order to get support.

Create offerings that speak to:

- High-growth tech founders;

- Solo freelancers and consultants;

- Creatives and makers;

- Neighborhood brick-and-mortar owners.

Tailored programming builds trust. It shows you see *them* and not just their business plan.

Build Regular Storytelling Into Your Outreach Strategy

When it comes to ecosystem building, visibility is more than just marketing. It's culture-building. When you spotlight founders, you're not just sharing a win. You're sending a message that entrepreneurship matters here.

Try doing the following to help highlight the things happening in your community:

- Monthly founder features in local media;

- Behind-the-scenes videos from events or workspaces;

- "Why I Build Here" social posts from local entrepreneurs.

At times, it may feel like you're hyping your community. But that's not why you're doing it. You're building belonging. You're showing entrepreneurs that there are people just like them, people with the same struggles and the same ambitions, right in their backyard.

Recruit Boomerang Founders and Remote Workers With Targeted Campaigns

Some of your strongest future founders already know your city. They grew up there. Went to college nearby. Moved away but might be ready to return. You just have to give them a reason to come back.

Others are looking for places that offer:

- Lower cost of living;

- Greater quality of life;

- Tight-knit, supportive communities.

Don't just pitch amenities. Pitch alignment. Show how your city supports real builders and not just tourists.

Offer Small-Dollar Microgrants and "Office Hours" for Key Services

Founders don't need red tape. What they need is runway.

Seed the next wave of innovation by providing:

- Microgrants ($500–$2,500) to test ideas or launch MVPs;

- Free office hours with legal, financial, and marketing pros;

- Access to templates, tools, and city-specific startup checklists.

These are small investments that can make a big difference.

Reduce Bureaucratic Friction (Licenses, Permits, Compliance)

You can't say you support entrepreneurs if your permitting process takes six months.

Audit the red tape:

- How hard is it to register a business?

- Is your licensing process transparent and digital?

- Can new founders talk to a real person if they get stuck?

Every layer of complexity is a chance for momentum to die. Simplify everything you can.

Make It Easy to Say "Yes"

Founders don't expect handouts. But they do need clarity, access, and support that respects their time and ambition.

And don't stop there. Don't be afraid to borrow from improv comedy and start saying "Yes, and…." Let your founders know that your ecosystem appreciates their effort and is willing to go the extra mile to help them succeed. Because the more they hear "yes, and…," the more excited they get about launching their startup. The more momentum builds in your city. And the more powerful your ecosystem becomes.

This checklist isn't about checking boxes. It's about creating momentum, one founder, one win, and one story at a time.

Make Entrepreneurs Feel Seen

Let's put the technical language aside for a second. This isn't truly about ecosystems. It's not about programs, pitch nights, or portfolios of real estate. It's really about people.

It's about making a city where people with crazy ideas don't feel alone.

When a young founder walks into a room with what seems like a crazy concept and gets a nod instead of a raised eyebrow.

Where a parent with a side job feels like she's part of something bigger and not just tolerated but really embraced.

The first thing you should do if you want to aid and support entrepreneurs is let them know that you see them and appreciate what they do. Show them that you care about their time and goals and that you respect them. Make sure they feel like they are part of something special and connected. That they know who to call and where to go. And that they feel ready for the task of starting their entrepreneurial journey, not scared by it.

That doesn't happen through chance. It happens through intentional design, through the way you build programs, host events, tell stories, and respond when someone says, "I've got an idea."

If your city can do that for dozens or even hundreds of founders, you won't just grow a startup scene. You'll shift the culture of what's possible. You'll create a place where innovation doesn't have to be imported. It's homegrown.

And that's when the real transformation begins.

PART IV

FUELING PRIORITIES AND TRACKING PROGRESS

CHAPTER 7:
FUNDING THE ECOSYSTEM

Access to funding is an important part of starting a business and a key part of building an ecosystem. But where you live has a direct effect on the availability of funds. For instance, despite accounting for just 44 percent of the U.S. population, startups located in the top 50 MSAs account for a disproportionate share of investment capital. By most accounts, businesses in these MSAs receive 97 percent of all VC funding. That means entrepreneurs in the other half of the country, the small cities and rural markets, are only able to capture three percent of VC funds. That's it. Just three percent.

When you realize that, it's easy to see why the narrative of having to move to the coastal communities or big markets is so pervasive.

So, here you are trying to excite your residents to launch the next big thing. To think outside the proverbial box. To be bold. And to do it, knowing that they'll struggle to gain access to most of the VC funding available.

But here's the good news: you don't need Silicon Valley money to build a meaningful, thriving ecosystem.

What you need is a realistic plan, a diverse set of funding sources, and a long-term mindset. Not just to support your startups, but to invest in the scaffolding that will hold your ecosystem together. The programs, the places, and the people.

This chapter is your roadmap.

In this chapter, we'll unpack:

- Where ecosystem funding can come from (and where it usually doesn't);

- How to fund infrastructure without chasing every shiny grant;

- Why local investment matters more than you think;

- And how to build a funding model that's sustainable, inclusive, and aligned with your community's values.

In the context of building a startup ecosystem, funding tends to follow momentum. Funders invest in what they can see, measure, and believe in. If you can prove that your ecosystem is more than a buzzword and that you're building a movement, they'll want to join.

So yes, let's talk money.

But let's also talk ownership, sustainability, and shared commitment. Because if you're going to build something that lasts, you'll need more than just dollars. You'll need belief, conviction, and a plan to back it up.

First: Redefine What "Funding" Means

When people hear the word "funding," the conversation almost always goes straight to two places. One, "Can we land a big federal grant?" Or two, "Can we attract some angel investors?"

And sure, those things matter. Money matters. But if that's the only definition of funding your ecosystem is operating with, you're missing 75 percent of the equation.

Thriving ecosystems are fueled by more than just money. It takes all kinds of capital to bring your ecosystem to life, and money is just part of it.

Think of capital as having four forms:

- **Financial Capital**

   Yes, money. This one is obvious. These are the grants, sponsorships, investments, budget allocations, and other forms of financial support that can help offset infrastructure and programming costs. Yes, it's important. But it's not the only resource that keeps an ecosystem alive.

- **Social Capital**

   Who picks up the phone when you call? Who invites whom to the table? This manifests itself in the form of trust, networks, and mentorship, all of the invisible things that reduce friction and move people forward. You can't buy this. You earn it over time.

- **Political Capital**

  These are the local elected officials, school boards, utility commissions, and economic development organizations. They might not be the ones writing checks, but they can open doors, remove roadblocks, and align policy with entrepreneurial goals. If they believe in the mission, things happen faster.

- **In-Kind Capital**

  This is the unsung hero of most ecosystems. When a local law firm or accounting firm offers free office hours. When a community college or university donates classroom space for a startup bootcamp. When a city employee dedicates five hours a week to ecosystem coordination. It all adds up, and it all has real value, even if it doesn't show up in your bank account.

The key is recognizing and valuing all four forms of capital and then finding ways to align them. Because the best ecosystems don't just raise money; they build shared commitment.

And sometimes you'll find that you don't need more cash. You just need better coordination.

If one organization is sitting on underused space and another has a team of volunteers but no venue, then your problem isn't funding. It's fragmentation.

So before you chase the next big grant or wait for a VC to return your call, ask:

- What assets already exist in this community?

- Who's quietly supporting this work, even if it's unofficial?

- How can we leverage trust, relationships, and shared vision as currencies, too?

Because once you broaden your definition of "funding," you find more than money.

You find real momentum.

Start With Institutional Anchors

When people ask, "Where's the money going to come from?" I generally encourage them to simply look around.

Not every small city will be able to tap into a $100 million grant like Augusta. If you can, great! If not? Don't worry about it. Because some of your most important funders are already in your zip code. And no, I'm not just talking about private investors or national grant programs. I'm talking about your institutional anchors. Those organizations that already shape your community's economic, civic, and educational landscape.

These aren't new players. They've been here. They're trusted. And most importantly, they're already invested in your community's success.

These are the:

- **City or county government**—with workforce, small business, or community development budgets already on the books;

- Universities and technical colleges—often sitting on space, staff, curriculum, and research talent waiting to be aligned;

- Chambers of commerce—with networks of small business owners and an interest in job creation;

- Local banks and credit unions—who may not fund tech unicorns but are often eager to support local entrepreneurship with microgrants, sponsorships, or community reinvestment dollars;

- Economic development organizations (EDOs) — looking to diversify their region's job base beyond industrial recruitment;

- Community foundations—especially those with a mission around equity, youth, or economic mobility.

These institutions don't have to become the ecosystem. But they can and should invest in it.

And that investment doesn't always look like a giant check.

Sometimes it's:

- A $10,000 budget line from a university to pilot a student founder initiative;

- A city government offering up a vacant building rent-free for a startup hub;

- A chamber staff member dedicating 10 hours a month to ecosystem convening;

- A foundation underwriting childcare for entrepreneurs attending evening workshops.

These small, strategic moves often do more to sustain an ecosystem than a one-time $100K grant from the outside. Why? Because they're rooted in local trust, aligned missions, and long-term presence.

But you have to connect the dots. Don't just walk into the mayor's office or a college president's boardroom talking about pitch competitions and accelerators. Instead, frame it like this:

- "This ecosystem effort can help you retain young talent."

- "We can support local job creation and economic diversification."

- "We're helping families build generational wealth through entrepreneurship."

- "This aligns with your strategic plan, your mission, and your metrics."

In other words, don't just ask for support; offer alignment.

When institutional anchors see ecosystem building not as your initiative but as a shared strategy that helps them achieve their goals, that's when the dollars, staff time, and real influence start showing up.

And remember that you're not just asking for funding; you're inviting them to co-own the future of your community's economy. That's a powerful ask and the start of a much stronger partnership.

Identify and Layer Funding Sources

When it comes to funding your ecosystem, I'm afraid there is no magic pot of money sitting somewhere waiting to be unlocked with the right pitch deck or grant application.

Startup ecosystems, especially in small and mid-sized cities, aren't built with a single check. They're built the same way entrepreneurs build businesses: by securing investments, soliciting support, and generating revenue.

You don't need one silver bullet. What you need is a layered strategy that includes a mix of funding sources that reinforce each other and reduce risk.

Here's how that can look.

1. Public Funding

- **City or County Budgets:** Economic development, workforce, or special tax allocation dollars can be aligned with entrepreneurial initiatives.

- **State Programs:** Look for small business innovation funds, rural revitalization grants, or sector-specific support (e.g. agtech, green energy).

- **Federal Opportunities:** Think SBA, EDA, USDA, and NSF. The alphabet soup of federal agencies offers programs that could be used by different members of your ecosystem to help build infrastructure and capacity. And these funds aren't just for big cities. According to the Urban Institute, rural areas receive more EDA funding on a per capita basis than urban areas, $37 vs. $13, respectively. So log on to grants.gov, monitor what's available, and check the eligibility for each funding opportunity.

- **Workforce Boards:** Often overlooked, they may fund training programs that align with the startup or gig economy. Many workforce boards utilize funding from the Workforce Innovation and Opportunity Act to support entrepreneurial skills training. And if yours doesn't? Talk to them and area service providers about making a change.

2. Philanthropic and Foundation Support

- **Community Foundations:** Especially when your goals align with equity, education, or youth entrepreneurship.

- **Regional or National Foundations:** Some of the big players in this space are the Ewing Marion Kauffman Foundation, the Blackstone Charitable Foundation, the Skoll Foundation, or local health-focused foundations willing to invest in upstream economic solutions.

- **Faith-based or Civic Organizations:** They may not have large grants, but they often fund initiatives that uplift marginalized communities.

3. Corporate Sponsorships and Corporate Social Responsibility Funds

Local banks, healthcare systems, utilities, and even manufacturers often have budgets for community impact or workforce development. What they lack is a mechanism to plug in.

Position your ecosystem initiatives as:

- Workforce pipelines;

- Supplier diversity incubators;

- Entrepreneurial upskilling efforts tied to their industries.

Remember, these companies aren't just investing in your program. They're investing in efforts that lead to a stronger local economy, which ultimately benefits them too.

4. Earned Revenue and Fee-for-Service

Don't ignore revenue-generating opportunities:

- Nominal coworking or event fees;

- Sliding-scale memberships for access to mentorship or a makerspace;

- Corporate training or licensing of ecosystem-developed curriculum;

- University partnerships where credit or certificates generate tuition revenue.

Even small, predictable revenue streams create stability and credibility.

5. In-Kind and Sweat Equity

Every dollar you don't have to spend is a dollar you can reinvest somewhere else. It's also an opportunity to generate additional buy-in from organizations that may not have the financial means to cut a check. Don't overlook:

- Donated space;

- Volunteer mentors;

- University interns;

- Loaned staff time from partner organizations;

- Free marketing via local media or city channels.

Regardless of the source of capital, always be sure to count it. Track it. Leverage it.

The Key: Stack Strategically

The best-funded ecosystems don't chase every grant. Instead, they align capital with their core priorities. They know when to say yes, when to say no, and how to match the right funding source to the right type of work.

Example:

- Use public funds to cover infrastructure and staffing.

- Use private dollars for founder-focused microgrants or flexible programming.

- Use in-kind support for operations, mentorship, and space.

This layered model doesn't just create financial sustainability. It builds resilience in programs and your ecosystem; if one funding stream dries up, the ecosystem keeps moving.

So when it comes to building an ecosystem that will last, don't overly concentrate on finding a single source of capital. Think diversification. Because the most enduring ecosystems aren't funded once. They're continuously supported by a community that believes in the work.

Here are some common sources of financial capital to consider:

Funding Source	Use Case	Tips
City/County Budgets	Staff support, space, microgrants	Tie to small business or workforce goals

Federal Grants	Programs, infrastructure	Check EDA, SBA, USDA, and NSF programs
Philanthropy	Inclusive entrepreneurship efforts	Focus on equity, youth, or rural development
Corporate Sponsors	Events, accelerators, prizes	Align with marketing or talent pipeline needs
University Funding	Student ventures, research, space	Embed in curriculum or innovation centers
Membership/ Fees	Coworking, workshops, events	Keep affordable; use sliding scales
Revenue-Share Models	Program sustainability	Take small equity or revenue % from graduates
Investment Funds	High-growth startup capital	Often requires separate limited partner or angel network setup

The key is stacking funding across partners so that no single entity is overburdened.

Demonstrate Value Early and Often

I cannot overstate the importance of demonstrating value to your supporters, letting them know what you did with their support and how much momentum they're helping you generate. But value isn't something you just talk about. It's something you have to prove. And not just at the time a report is due. You have to prove it consistently and publicly.

It doesn't mean a startup has to raise a $5 million Series A round or land on the cover of *Fortune*. But if you want sustained investment, you have to show that what you're building is working. Not just for one founder, but for the entire community.

What You Measure Matters

There are two primary ways that you can help demonstrate value, and both will be discussed in subsequent chapters. These are quantitative and qualitative.

When it comes to quantitative reporting, the key is to capture and report metrics that speak to funders. Forget vanity metrics. Focus on the indicators that speak to impact and momentum. Chapter 8 is dedicated to the importance of metrics, but for now, start with these basic numbers:

- **Startups Launched:** Are new ventures being formed? How many came through your programs, pitch nights, or mentorship circles?

- **Jobs Created:** Report these in terms of Full-Time Equivalency (FTE). That means that even part-time or contract gigs count. Every new paycheck is a signal that entrepreneurship is becoming a real economic engine in your city.

- **Revenue and Capital Raised:** Whether it's $500 from a first sale or $50,000 in seed investment, track it. Report it. Celebrate it.

- **Underrepresented Founders Supported:** This is critical. Funders want to know you're reaching women, people of color, rural residents, veterans, and others often excluded from innovation conversations.

- **Student Ventures Piloted:** Are young people getting involved? Starting something? Even if it fails, it counts.

- **Programs Delivered:** I'm not just talking about how many programs, but also about their relevance. Did they move the needle for the participants?

- **Community Events Hosted:** Gatherings matter. They create culture and visibility. And their mere occurrence sends a message to the broader community that things are happening. Don't just tally the events. Keep a count of how many people and highlight who they are and why they're there.

Don't Just Track It—Tell the Story

Metrics and results are only part of the equation. Data are the foundation. Narrative is the amplifier. For every number you track, pair it with a face, a voice, or a quote. Don't just tell funders what happened; make sure to tell them who it happened for.

Chapter 11 provides a more detailed discussion of the impact of storytelling, but here are a few examples of storytelling in action:

- "Four students from a local HBCU win $25,000 in a statewide collegiate competition for a retractable extension cord idea."

- "An elementary student wins a $5,000 prize to develop his self-balancing bike concept to help other kids learn how to ride a bike."

- "Two young founders with an innovative new pool cleaning technology connect with a new sustainable incubator through a mentoring connection."

Package the Progress

Telling your funders and the public what's happening is a continuous process. Don't wait for a year-end report. Build a habit of consistent, bite-sized storytelling. Make it a point to develop:

- Monthly or quarterly "impact snapshots;"

- A running dashboard on your ecosystem webpage;

- Infographics for social media;

- Short video testimonials from founders and partners.

It's key to remember that you're not just reporting outcomes. You're building credibility. You're showing that investments in your ecosystem are moving the needle. And you're telling your funders that your efforts are worth reinvesting in.

Metrics Build Momentum

Just like startups, ecosystems earn investment by showing traction. So measure what matters. Share it often. And never assume people know the value of your work. You have to show them. Because when funders see real outcomes, they don't just open their wallets. They become champions of the movement.

And as you are talking to funders and building momentum, make it a point to involve entrepreneurs in the funding conversation. That's because you can't build for entrepreneurs without building with entrepreneurs.

Too often, funding conversations happen in boardrooms and budget meetings without a single founder in the room. That's a mistake because if the people you're trying to serve aren't part of the discussion, you risk investing in the wrong things or, worse, building something no one asked for.

Make Founders Part of the Process

Entrepreneurs aren't just beneficiaries of what you're creating. They're also builders. They are the ones that embody creativity, resourcefulness, and a knack for problem-solving. Treat them with respect and lean on their expertise.

Invite them to the table:

- Ask them to serve on advisory boards and grant review panels. Let founders help prioritize how dollars are spent. They'll spot blind spots and offer practical insight into what actually moves the needle.

- Make them a part of the feedback loops for program design. Before launching a new accelerator or mentorship series, ask: Would you use this? Would you recommend this?

- Seek their input during the budget review cycles. Especially in public-private partnerships, make sure the founders' voice is there to help assess ROI.

This isn't about giving veto power. It's about giving them a voice and honoring the reality that entrepreneurs are the experts in their own journey.

Create Founder-Centered Funding Models

A mature ecosystem doesn't just ask how it can serve founders. It also asks how founders can serve the next wave of founders. That's where give-back models come in. Two that work especially well in small cities and rural markets. They are founders' circles and pay-it-forward models.

1. Founders' Circles

An invite-only group of successful local entrepreneurs who:

- Contribute to a shared fund (monthly, quarterly, or annually);

- Provide feedback on how the funds are used;

- Offer mentorship, introductions, and event participation.

This builds both capital and credibility and sends a strong signal that your city believes in local reinvestment.

2. Pay-It-Forward Models

Instead of asking early-stage founders to pay cash, ask for their time instead. Next time:

- Grant access to a free accelerator in exchange for their willingness to mentor the next cohort.

- If they're a microgrant recipient, ask them to host one free workshop the next year.

- If you provide a scholarship for a coworking space, ask them to volunteer at a pitch night or demo day.

This works because it turns "help" into reciprocity and keeps the ecosystem rooted in relationships, not just transactions.

Why It's Important

Involving entrepreneurs in funding decisions does three things:

1. **Builds trust:** Founders see that the system values their perspective.

2. **Improves impact:** Resources get aligned with real needs, not assumptions.

3. **Creates sustainability:** Today's founders become tomorrow's funders, mentors, and champions.

That's how ecosystems become self-reinforcing.

Not by chasing new money every year—but by creating cycles of value, contribution, and renewal.

Empowerment Is the ROI

When you give entrepreneurs a say in how the ecosystem grows, you're not just empowering individuals, you're institutionalizing respect. You're also signaling that their voice matters. Not just at the pitch table, but at the strategy table. And in the long run, that sense of shared ownership is worth more than any single grant.

It's what turns short-term wins into long-term momentum.

Avoid These Pitfalls: Funding Without Focus Can Derail Everything

Make no mistake about it, money helps. But only when it's aligned with what you're trying to build. I've seen promising ecosystems stall, not from lack of hustle or passion, but from funding decisions that seemed smart in the short term, only to end up costly in the long run.

Even well-intentioned dollars can do more harm than good if they're chasing the wrong priorities, disconnected from partners, or built on unsustainable models.

As you develop your funding strategy, below are four common traps to watch for and how to avoid them.

1. Grant-Chasing Without a Strategy

It's tempting. A federal grant opportunity opens up with six-figure potential, and suddenly everyone's pivoting their mission to fit the application.

Don't do it.

If the funding doesn't serve your actual goals, the ones defined by your community, your founders, and your local context, then don't waste your precious time, energy, and goodwill pursuing it. Because in the end, you're not growing your ecosystem. You're simply growing your inbox and burning out your team. A better approach would be to build your strategic plan first. Let your goals dictate your funding targets, not the other way around.

2. Siloed Fundraising Across Partners

Here's something that happens more often than you would think. Three local organizations see a grant opportunity and submit for three separate grants. Each only slightly different from the other. They don't talk to each other. Funders that might have been inclined to support the area now get confused. What they see is duplication and a lack of alignment. Everyone loses credibility.

A better approach would be to create a shared funding calendar or convene a quarterly "development huddle." Coordinate applications, align asks, and when possible, submit joint proposals. Funders love leverage and cooperation.

3. Overfunding Without Accountability

It sounds counterintuitive, but too much money without a clear purpose or tracking can actually slow progress.

I've seen cities land $500,000 grants and spend 18 months figuring out how to use them. Meanwhile, the entrepreneurs who needed help yesterday are still waiting.

Money without a feedback loop can lead to programs with no participants, spaces with no energy, and staff with no sense of urgency. A better approach would be to tie funding to clear milestones. Track participation, outcomes, and learning. Build a rhythm of accountability into every grant or sponsorship agreement, not just the ones that mandate it.

4. Ignoring Long-Term Sustainability

Building an ecosystem that will last is the goal, and you shouldn't lose sight of that. So, that pilot program you just launched with a $50,000 grant? What happens when that funding runs out?

If your answer is "we'll figure it out later," you've already started the clock on a future failure.

Every ecosystem program, no matter the size, needs a sustainability plan. That doesn't always mean full self-sufficiency, but it does mean clarity. You should always be thinking toward the future. When you launch that new program, you need to be asking:

- Will this be absorbed by a partner institution?

- Can it be sustained through fee-for-service?

- Is it a one-time intervention by design?

A better approach is to design every initiative with a "sunset or sustain" question in mind from day one. Don't assume you'll always find more dollars. Plan like you won't and be ready to answer what comes after.

Fund With Foresight, Not Just Urgency

Ecosystem building is full of momentum and emotion, but when it comes to funding, discipline matters. Chasing dollars for the sake of optics, or letting urgency outrun strategy, will only leave you scrambling. The ecosystems that thrive financially aren't the ones with the biggest grants. They're the ones with clarity, coordination, accountability, and a plan for what comes next.

That's how you turn dollars into impact and impact into lasting change.

Meet Skip—Real World Example

I still remember the first time I met Skip. He was the dean of a college of business in Brunswick, Georgia, and had read about some of the things that I was doing in ecosystem building. We initially touched base over the phone, and it didn't take long for me to invite him over for a tour and to chat.

When we connected, Skip spoke about Brunswick with a contagious pride. He spoke glowingly about the entrepreneurs in the city and the potential he saw in his students. He talked about how many successful retirees there were and how eager they were to help shape the next generation. But he also shared that he felt that something was missing. Skip thought there wasn't a central place where people could gather to share ideas, find resources, and work together.

That made sense to me. I had seen similar gaps in other small cities, and I knew the impact a dedicated entrepreneurial hub could make. Not long after, Skip invited me to Brunswick. We walked the city together, talked with business owners, met with community leaders, and toured spaces on and off the college campus that could be transformed. Together, we began imagining a place that wasn't just a building but a living network that would integrate education, entrepreneurship, and economic development.

It took a while for Skip to bring that vision to life, but once he did, it took root quickly. While he always kept an eye out for a physical space, he didn't let the absence of a location slow his momentum. He built community.

Skip brought together the right people and cultivated relationships with donors whose values aligned with the mission. He would talk about the importance of entrepreneurship with anyone who would listen. He read about it in the local newspaper. He would lead monthly coffee and conversation-style events at a popular local bar before the crew started their lunch shift.

His persistence eventually led to funding. Art Lucas, a successful entrepreneur, had sold his company and returned to his roots. He had been supportive of what Skip was trying to build and was a strong believer in using entrepreneurship as a retention strategy. He was just waiting for the right moment. The right opportunity to step into the ecosystem conversation. Eventually, he saw what Skip had accomplished. He saw his passion. He saw its legitimacy. And the Lucas Center for Entrepreneurship was born.

When the doors opened, the energy was palpable. Students worked on business ideas with mentors from the community. Local entrepreneurs used the space to refine their strategies and grow their companies. Workshops, pitch events, idea bootcamps, and collaborative projects began to fill the calendar.

It started with a small space in the business building, hired a dedicated director, and then moved to a downtown location to be better connected with their city's founders. And in the process, the Lucas Center became more than a facility; it became a hub of possibility.

Action Checklist: Funding Your Ecosystem Intentionally and Sustainably

To be clear, building a startup ecosystem isn't about finding one big pot of money. It's about assembling a mosaic of resources. It's about pulling all forms of capital (i.e., financial, social, political, and in-kind) that collectively power long-term growth.

If you want to fund your ecosystem with purpose, use this checklist as your guide:

Inventory All Potential Institutional and Philanthropic Partners

Before you chase external grants, take stock of the allies already in your backyard.

- Who has a mission aligned with ecosystem development?

- Which universities, chambers, foundations, or anchor institutions have capacity, financial or otherwise, to contribute to the ecosystem?

- What local employers might support entrepreneurship as part of a workforce or supplier development strategy?

Think beyond dollars. Think space, staff time, and political support. They all count.

Create a Shared Funding Pitch That Ties to Economic Goals

Funders, particularly public entities, want to know what impact their investment is having. They want to know if they're helping move the needle. And they want to know if the results are aligned with their investment goals.

So don't just talk about the number of startups you're assisting or the amount of capital you're helping them raise. Talk about the impact your ecosystem is having on job creation, the difference you're making in retaining youth, and the things you're doing to make your city more resilient.

Crafting a narrative that is co-created with your partners and helps turn fragmented asks into a coordinated movement.

Stack Multiple Funding Types Across Different Sources

Think like a portfolio manager. Don't hang all your hopes, dreams, and future on a single funding source. Make sure your revenue stream is diversified and balanced. Be sure to blend:

- Public dollars (city, county, state, federal);

- Philanthropic grants (foundations, donor-advised funds);

- Corporate sponsorships (local banks, utilities, hospitals);

- In-kind contributions (space, services, equipment);

- Earned revenue (membership fees, paid workshops).

No single source should carry the entire load. Diversify for stability.

Track and Report Key Metrics Regularly to Funders

Your funders are your stakeholders and need to be treated like it. Don't wait for a grant report or when you need additional funding. Be consistent in letting them know what you are up to. Share monthly or quarterly updates and be active in celebrating wins and conveying what you're learning. Furthermore, don't just count heads in the room. Track the outcomes that matter most to your funders and that best tell your impact: startups launched, jobs created, dollars leveraged.

Transparency builds trust. And trust builds long-term investment.

Start with Pilot Initiatives and Grow Based on Success

When it comes to resource allocation, don't overbuild. And don't overspend. Start with something lean and high-impact, then prove its value. Launch a startup weekend event for students or a six-week founder bootcamp. Host quarterly mentor office hours or run a mini-grant program for underrepresented founders. Focus on getting results. Then work on taking it to scale.

Explore Earned Revenue or "Give-Back" Models From Founders

Sustainability doesn't have to mean dependency. Some ecosystems charge nominal coworking fees or event registrations.

This helps ensure that clients have skin in the game and are committed to attending. Others utilize build "pay-it-forward" programs that are free to join and require participants to give back later or invite successful founders to sponsor new programs or mentor cohorts. When founders succeed, invite them to reinvest in the ecosystem that supported them. Find the right mix of support that works for your founders and your community.

Involve Entrepreneurs in Funding Strategy and Governance

If entrepreneurs aren't in the room, you're building around them, not with them. Utilize their expertise as problem-solvers and builders. Include them on advisory boards, and let them help shape funding priorities. Ask what support they'd actually pay for or commit time toward, and work with them to structure programs they value.

The ecosystem is for them. Make sure it's shaped by them.

Your goal isn't to patch together a few good programs and make it look like an ecosystem. Your goal is to build an engine of entrepreneurship that runs on community trust, aligned investment, and shared ownership. Use this checklist not just to raise money but to build a funding culture in your ecosystem that is rooted in intentionality, transparency, and a long-term vision.

That's how you make your ecosystem resilient and authentic.

Money Follows Meaning

Finally, when it comes to funding, don't fall into the trap of thinking that, "If we just had more money, we could build a great ecosystem." This line of thinking undervalues what you've accomplished and will kill your momentum. And it's simply not true.

When it comes to building a thriving startup community, whether it was a mid-sized Southern town or a rural hub finding its footing, money didn't lead the movement. Meaning did.

When entrepreneurs feel seen, when programs solve real problems, and when spaces hum with creative energy, that's when funders take notice. And not because you chased them down with a glossy pitch deck. But because the work speaks for itself.

Just as in the case of the Lucas Center, money will come when you have:

- **Clarity of vision:** When your community knows what it's building and why;

- **Alignment of action:** When partners work together instead of in silos;

- **Visible traction:** When founders succeed and their stories get told;

- **Trust in leaders:** When your ecosystem shows consistency, not just offers lip service.

Funders don't want vanity metrics. They want value. And they want to see that you're building something that lasts.

So yes, keep building your funding strategy. Keep pitching and partnering and tracking outcomes, but don't let money become the mission.

Build something meaningful. Make the impact undeniable, and the money will follow. Not because you asked for it, but because you earned it.

That's how small cities become startup cities. Not through capital campaigns alone, but through a culture that creates its own energy. Its own momentum.

And that's where real, sustainable transformation begins.

CHAPTER 8:
MEASURING WHAT MATTERS

---

*"You cannot manage what you cannot measure…
and what gets measured gets done."*

-Bill Hewlett, *co-founder, Hewlett Packard*

Metrics are a tricky business. They can shine a light on your efforts or just as easily cast a shadow on your work. They can help drive progress or just as easily distract from it. And in the world of ecosystem building, I've seen both happen.

On the one hand, data are critical. You can't build a thriving startup community on vibes alone. You need to know what's working, where the gaps are, and how to make the case for sustained investment. Funders want to see outcomes. Stakeholders want to see movement. Entrepreneurs want to know that their time and effort aren't being wasted. But not all metrics are created equal.

Too many communities fall into the trap of chasing easy wins, the big attendance numbers, social media likes, or the number of workshops hosted as if those alone signify success. They don't. Not if no new companies are being launched. Not if underrepresented founders are still stuck on the sidelines. Not if the community feels just as fragmented as it did before.

This chapter is about clarity. It's about choosing metrics that reflect actual transformation, not just activity. It's about measuring forward momentum, not just motion.

We'll explore:

- Which metrics matter for different phases of ecosystem growth;

- How to collect and report data in ways that build trust;

- Why qualitative wins are just as valuable as quantitative ones;

- How to align your tracking with your values, not just your vanity.

You want to keep in mind that the metrics you track will shape the behavior of your ecosystem. If you reward volume, you'll get volume. If you reward depth, equity, and sustainability, then you'll build something that lasts. So it's not enough to simply talk about numbers; you need to make sure that what you're tracking is telling the right story.

Start With the Why: Clarify the Mission Before You Measure

Before you pull out the spreadsheets, before you pick KPIs, before you chase benchmarks from other cities, I want you to pause and ask, "What are we actually trying to accomplish?"

It sounds obvious, but you'd be surprised how many ecosystems start tracking things without ever defining success for themselves. They measure what's easy, what looks good, or what someone else told them to track.

If you don't align your metrics to your mission, then you're just creating noise. Measurement has to begin with meaning. It has to be anchored in the specific outcomes your community cares about. Before you start chasing numbers, you need to be very clear on your goal. Ask yourself:

- Are we attempting to help more people start their own businesses?

- Are we focused on helping current startups develop and become bigger?

- Are we dedicated to helping founders who aren't well-represented in typical startup spaces?

- Is it our purpose to keep young people who might depart for bigger cities?

- Do we want to create a unique identity for innovation that is based on the strengths and values of our area?

Each of these goals requires a different approach and a different set of indicators to track.

This step can't be skipped or outsourced. If you don't know what you're aiming for, then any metric will do, and that's a dangerous place to be. You might end up designing programs that fill rooms but don't change lives. Or you might pour energy into initiatives that look innovative but don't serve your people.

So slow down. Get aligned. Define success on your own terms. Because once you know what matters, you can start measuring what moves the needle.

The Three Layers of Measurement: Beyond the Numbers That Look Good

Too often, we fixate on just a few numbers, like startups launched or dollars raised, and end up ignoring the full ecosystem story. If you want to get a real sense of how your startup ecosystem's performing, you have to look beyond surface metrics. That's because ecosystems are multi-layered. There's not a single data point that measures its health or your progress.

Ecosystems are made up of a series of actions and support systems, all intertwined and all with different metrics. So, when it comes to measurement, think in three interconnected tiers:

1. Startup-Level Metrics: Your Bottom Line

This is where most people start and where many funders focus. These are the tangible, results-driven numbers tied directly to founder and business performance:

- Number of startups launched;
- Jobs created or retained;
- Capital raised (grants, loans, equity);
- Revenue growth;
- Customer traction or corporate pilots;
- Business survival rates at 1, 3, and 5 years.

These are your ecosystem's outcomes. They reflect the effectiveness of your support systems, but they don't tell the whole story. They're the tip of the iceberg, not the mass beneath the surface.

2. Program-Level Metrics: Your Leading Indicators

Strong startup metrics are usually built on strong programs. This second layer measures how well your initiatives are functioning and whether they're actually creating the conditions for growth:

- Event attendance and repeat participation;

- Applications to incubators, accelerators, or training programs;

- Participant satisfaction scores and qualitative feedback;

- Microgrant dollars disbursed and tracked;

- Mentor or adviser engagement hours logged.

These are the day-to-day levers you can pull. They won't impress everyone at city hall, but they're how you get to the results that do. They show traction and help keep things moving in the right direction over time.

3. Ecosystem-Level Metrics: Your Culture

This third layer is the hardest to measure, but it might be the most powerful. These measures show how well you are really creating an atmosphere that recognizes, supports, and keeps entrepreneurship going throughout time:

- Entrepreneurial sentiment and perception assessed via surveys or interviews;

- Collaboration across sectors (joint projects, events held together, referrals);

- Diversity and inclusion (race, gender, where you live, and your financial background);

- Keeping and bringing back talent (particularly among students and young professionals);

- More coworking spaces, investment groups, and programs being built in the ecosystem.

These indicators take longer to shift, and they don't always show up in annual reports. But if they're moving in the right direction, it means your city is becoming a place where entrepreneurship is no longer a pipe dream; it's becoming normalized.

If you only track startup success, you miss the early warning signs. If you only measure programs, you lose sight of impact. If you ignore culture, you'll never shift the narrative of what's possible in your community. Strong ecosystems measure all three. Because metrics aren't just for reporting what you did; they're for learning, adjusting, and growing with purpose.

Avoid Vanity Metrics: Impress Less, Learn More

Every ecosystem, especially in the early days, is tempted by numbers that look impressive but don't actually move the needle. We chase the headline: "500 RSVPs!" "10,000 website hits!" "1,000 Instagram followers!" And while those numbers might win you applause, they won't build an ecosystem.

Vanity metrics confuse motion with meaning. They can inflate your confidence while quietly deflating your progress.

Let's break down a few common issues with using vanity metrics:

Social Media Followers

Ten thousand followers mean nothing if none of them are local, engaged, or actually participating in your programs. Community isn't measured by likes. It's measured by trust and action.

Event RSVPs (Without Show-Up Rates)

We've all been there. We have a large number of RSVPs but a half-empty room. Attendance matters. Engagement matters. If you're not tracking who actually shows up and whether they return, then you're flying blind.

Dollars Requested vs. Dollars Secured

Big grant applications sound bold, but money requested isn't money received and definitely not money well spent. Focus on what's awarded, deployed, and producing results.

Website Traffic Without Conversion

High traffic is only helpful if it leads to something meaningful, such as event registrations, program applications, or mentor sign-ups. If your homepage gets 1,000 views a month but no one takes the next step, the metric is noise.

Use With Caution

Now, are vanity metrics always useless? Not necessarily. They can serve a role, especially when it comes to helping you assess your awareness or reach. But they should never be the metrics that shape strategy, justify funding, or evaluate impact.

So how do you know if you're tracking a vanity metric? Here's the test. If a number sounds impressive, ask, "So what?"

- Did it change behavior?

- Did it create value?

- Did it move someone from interest to action?

If not, put it in the footnotes, not the headlines.

Focus on the numbers that make your community smarter, more responsive, and better equipped to serve real entrepreneurs. Because real impact doesn't always look sexy in a tweet. But it does change lives. And that's the metric that truly matters.

Create a Simple Dashboard: Clarity Over Complexity

Data don't have to be complicated to be useful. I've seen too many communities fall into the trap of overengineering their metrics and building massive spreadsheets with color-coded cells, endless tabs, and KPIs that no one ever looks at (let alone understands). The result? Analysis paralysis. You end up tracking everything and learning nothing.

It would be a far better approach to create a simple, focused dashboard that tracks real movement and can be updated. Not vanity. Not fluff. Just the numbers that help your ecosystem make smarter decisions.

Pick 8–10 Metrics That Matter

That's it. Not 25. Not 50. Eight to ten metrics that your team can rally around, communicate clearly, and use to course-correct when needed. A good dashboard balances across the three levels of ecosystem measurement:

1. Startup-Level (Outcomes)

- Number of new businesses started;

- Jobs created or retained;

- Capital raised (loans, grants, equity);

- Revenue milestones reached.

2. Program-Level (Engagement & Quality)

- Training program completions;

- Event attendance (with demographics);

- Mentor hours logged;

- Founder satisfaction scores or testimonials.

3. Ecosystem-Level (Culture & Connectivity)

- Number of ecosystem partners collaborating;

- Diversity of participants (race, gender, background);

- Talent retention (student or founder "stickiness").

Make sure that you are building something that your ecosystem will use. Not just something to be admired. That means don't design a dashboard that looks good in a boardroom but gathers dust between meetings. Build it to be:

- Updated quarterly;

- Shared publicly or with stakeholders;

- Discussed at leadership meetings;

- Is actionable; if a number dips, someone needs to own the response.

Make it visual. Make it clear. And above all, make it matter.

> **Bonus Tip: Include a "Win of the Quarter"**
>
> Metrics are critical, but don't forget the story. Add a simple callout each quarter for a key win. When you talk about the amount of capital that you helped startups raise, be sure to mention the local founder who closed a $50,000 seed round after participating in your mentorship program. And when you report on the number of startups that you assisted that quarter, talk about the three high schoolers that launched a mobile app during a summer bootcamp.
>
> These vignettes breathe life into your numbers and remind everyone why this work matters.

A dashboard isn't just a report; it's a compass. It tells you what direction your ecosystem is moving in. Keep it simple,. smart, and in service of the mission. And remember that you don't need perfect data to make progress. You just need the right data to stay on course.

Far too often, communities treat metrics like a final grade—pass or fail, success or bust. But real ecosystems don't operate like report cards. They behave more like living labs. The strongest startup ecosystems aren't just measuring what happened. They're learning from it. They create feedback loops that help foster smarter decisions, sharper programs, and deeper trust.

It's not just about finding out what worked; it's about asking:

- What did we learn?

- What surprised us?

- What should we change next time?

Learning Requires Deliberate Space

In the rush to plan the next event or pitch the next grant, learning often falls off the calendar. Don't let that happen. Build intentional moments for reflection into your ecosystem building rhythm:

- After every major program or event: Host a short debrief with staff, partners, and even participants. What worked? What didn't? What could be better next time?

- Quarterly with your ecosystem partners: Convene a "Learning Circle" to review what your metrics are saying and what they aren't. Yes, bring data, but also bring stories.

- Annually with the broader community: Open the books. Share the wins and the stumbles. Show that transparency is part of your DNA.

Use Data to Fuel Progress, Not Just Proof

Yes, funders want outcomes. And yes, public leaders want numbers. But don't stop there. Use data to ask better questions. For example:

- Participation was high—but did people come back?

- The program launched five new businesses—but did they reflect the demographics of your city?

- Event feedback was strong—but did anything change because of it?

This is how you build trust and stay relevant. Not by clinging to a perfect record, but by showing that you're learning faster than you're failing.

Capture Learning in Real Time

When it comes to learning, don't wait until the end of the year. Create a simple habit after every initiative of performing an after-action report. Don't overcomplicate it. Just one page, with three simple prompts:

1. What went well?

2. What didn't?

3. What will we change next time?

Even 15 minutes of reflection can yield insights that shift the entire trajectory of your ecosystem's efforts.

The important thing to remember is that success isn't static. It's iterative. The best ecosystems evolve not because they got it right the first time but because they kept learning fast enough to get it right the next time. So build a culture where measurement isn't just about milestones. It's about building momentum.

Share the Right Stories With the Right People

As you capture and report your activities, keep in mind that data open the door, but stories make people stay. In the world of ecosystem building, numbers give you legitimacy, but it's the stories that give you leverage. They humanize the work. They bring depth to your impact. And, most importantly, they remind your community, your funders, and your partners why this work matters.

Too often, we get caught up in reporting "30 new startups launched" or "$2.4 million in capital raised." Sure, those numbers matter. But they're not what people remember.

What they remember is the founder who bet on herself. The dad who built something for his kids to inherit. The college student who stayed in town because someone gave him a shot.

Tell stories that align with your mission. This isn't just about warm fuzzies. It's strategic. Your stories should reflect the values and priorities of your ecosystem. If you say you're focused on inclusive entrepreneurship, then highlight stories of diverse founders. If youth retention is a goal, tell the story of the student who stayed local to launch a tech startup.

Here are some examples of stories that move people:

- The high school senior who used a workforce development grant to launch a mobile car detailing service;

- The teacher who left school to join the college incubator graduated from the program and opened an interior design business in a formerly vacant downtown building;

- The immigrant entrepreneur who came from halfway around the world to start an online platform for processing rental payments and property maintenance agreements;

- The boomerang founder who left for college but returned to build in their hometown because they saw what was possible.

These aren't just anecdotes. They're anchors. They tether your ecosystem's outcomes to its values.

Match the Story to the Stakeholder

Just like metrics, stories work best when they're tailored to the audience. For instance:

- Funders want to hear about return on impact. Show how their dollars changed someone's trajectory.

- Elected officials want stories they can repeat on the campaign trail. Give them narratives that make them proud to support the work.

- The general public wants hope and possibility. Help them see that innovation isn't an abstract concept and that it's happening right here, in people they know.

- Entrepreneurs want to know they're not alone. Stories give them the courage to keep going.

To ensure you have the appropriate stories available when needed, begin compiling a continuous collection of founder stories, testimonials, and visuals. Make it easy to pull the right story at the right moment:

- Include a headshot and a one-paragraph backstory.

- Highlight the ecosystem touchpoints: What program helped them? Who mentored them? What milestone did they hit?

- Keep the stories fresh. Update them monthly or quarterly.

And better yet, invite entrepreneurs to tell their own stories. Use video. Use quotes. Use live events. Encourage them to post videos on their platforms that highlight their own entrepreneurial journey.

Always remember that data inform. Stories inspire. And the most effective ecosystems know how to use both. So go beyond spreadsheets. Shine a light on the lives being changed. Because in the end, no one falls in love with a metric. They fall in love with a mission.

And a well-told story is the shortest path to belief.

Action Checklist: Measuring What Matters

If you want to steer your ecosystem with clarity and not just activity, you need a simple, intentional measurement strategy. Not one built for press releases or board meetings, but one that helps you stay aligned with your mission, learn from your work, and communicate your impact in a way that resonates.

Here's a recap as to how to get started:

Define Your Ecosystem's Primary Purpose

Before you measure anything, get crystal clear on your "why." Are you here to help founders launch faster? Reduce brain drain? Build inclusive prosperity? If you don't define success in your own terms, someone else will, and you may end up chasing metrics that don't serve your community.

Identify 3–5 Startup-Level and Program-Level Metrics

Choose a small number of indicators that reflect real progress. Don't just think about attendance sheets or data that make you look good. Pay attention to:

- Startups launched;

- Jobs created or retained;

- Capital accessed;

- Repeat engagement in programs;

- Founder satisfaction or progress milestones.

Keep it small. Keep it focused. Let the numbers tell a story of traction—not just activity.

Add 2–3 Ecosystem-Level Indicators

These are harder to track—but they show whether the culture of entrepreneurship is taking root. Consider measuring:

- Founder diversity across gender, race, geography;

- Talent retention (who's staying to build?);

- Institutional collaboration (number of joint initiatives, shared grants, or partnerships).

Don't chase perfection here. Look for signals that your ecosystem is maturing and not just expanding.

Build a Shared Dashboard and Update It Quarterly

Put your metrics somewhere visible. There are dedicated platforms to assist in this, such as EcoMap Technologies, but this could be as simple as using Google Sheets, Airtable, a public-facing dashboard, or even a slide deck you review every quarter with ecosystem partners. This isn't just about accountability. It's about alignment.

A good dashboard does three things:

- Tracks what matters

- Sparks conversation

- Drives decision-making

Use retrospectives to adapt based on what you learn.

After every major program, pause. Reflect. Ask:

1. What worked?

2. What surprised us?

3. What needs to change next time?

Make it a habit. Quarterly retrospectives help you become a learning ecosystem and not just a doing one.

Pair metrics with founder stories to humanize the data.

No one falls in love with a number. People connect with people. Use storytelling to breathe life into your metrics:

- When you talk about the five new businesses you helped launch, tell the story of the mom who started a catering company.

- When you highlight the 15 jobs created, share how one founder hired two local teens and gave them their first paycheck.

The story is the proof. And when you connect it to your data, it turns numbers into meaning. You don't need 100 metrics. You need the right ones. Start small. Stay focused. And remember that what you measure will shape what you build.

PART V

GROWING AND SUSTAINING MOMENTUM

CHAPTER 9:
ENGAGING THE BROADER COMMUNITY

> *"Alone we can do so little; together we can do so much."*
>
> -Helen Keller, *author and educator*

One of the most persistent myths in startup ecosystem work is that if you've got founders, funders, and a few tech leaders, you're good to go. But that's not how real ecosystems grow. That's how they become echo chambers.

If you want your entrepreneurial ecosystem to last, then it has to be rooted in the life of your community. That means that it has to have broad appeal and deep meaning and be more inclusive than what you typically see out there. It has to reflect not just the business elite or the startup-savvy but the full spectrum of people who make your city what it is.

I'm talking about the middle school teacher helping kids create projects with a 3D printer.

The barber mentoring young men between haircuts.

The pastor providing leadership training to area youth.

The retiree who built three businesses and still reads the paper cover to cover.

The city worker who knows every empty building in town.

The parent juggling side gigs after bedtime.

These folks may never call themselves "entrepreneurs," but they embody the mindset every ecosystem needs. They provide the resourcefulness, resilience, and drive to make things better.

This chapter is about tapping into that energy. It's about expanding our definition of who belongs in the innovation conversation and making sure ecosystem building doesn't just happen for the community but with it. Inasmuch as you widen your circle and invite new voices to lead, you don't just create more buy-in. You create momentum that's real, rooted, and resilient.

Why Engagement Matters

If you want to build an ecosystem that lasts, you have to build one that belongs to more than just the insiders. It needs to include as many community voices as possible. Because when the broader community see themselves as active participants rather than just passive observers, everything changes.

Programs don't just fill seats; they fill with the right people, bringing energy, feedback, and lived experience that make those programs stronger and more grounded. Founders don't just get access to mentors and capital, they gain customers, champions, and cultural fluency. Policymakers don't just get policy memos, they get stories from their constituents, which makes them more likely to show up, fund up, and advocate. And funders, especially those local institutions who've been watching from the sidelines, start to see the ecosystem not as a risky bet but as a rising tide they can't afford to ignore.

Perhaps most critically, your ecosystem avoids the fate of so many others. It doesn't become an insular club of the already-connected, recycling the same names, same events, and same assumptions. It becomes porous. Dynamic. Alive.

Because at its best, a thriving ecosystem doesn't just serve startups. It serves the entire community. And a community that feels seen, heard, and valued? That's the kind that shows up. That votes with its dollars, time, trust, and talent.

So don't treat engagement as a side activity. It's not an outreach box to check. It's the difference between building something fleeting and building something enduring.

Who Are We Not Reaching?

Every ecosystem has blind spots. And the most effective way to find them isn't by patting ourselves on the back for who's in the room. It's by taking an honest look at who's not. Start by asking the question that often goes unspoken, "Who's missing and why?"

Because if your startup programs, pitch nights, or innovation centers are only attracting tech professionals, college students from one university, or a small circle of serial founders, then you've got a problem. You're not building an ecosystem. You're maintaining a clique.

Take a closer look at who's showing up. Are you reaching:

- Young professionals who left for bigger cities but might return if they saw a reason to;

- Seniors and retirees with decades of business experience, now sitting on the sidelines;

- Blue-collar workers, like welders, mechanics, truck drivers, those people who are solving real problems every day, but aren't part of the "innovation" conversation;

- Women and founders of color, who might be running thriving businesses in informal networks but feel excluded from formal startup circles;

- Neighborhoods beyond downtown, where the economic energy is real, even if the branding is missing;

- High schoolers, teachers, or first-gen college students, who haven't been shown what's possible;

- Artists and creatives that are building brands, crafting experiences, and molding microbusinesses, but are often overlooked as "serious" entrepreneurs.

These aren't fringe cases. These are your hidden assets. Your ecosystem's full potential won't be realized until they're part of the story. And not as tokens, but as co-creators.

Too often we assume people aren't showing up because they aren't interested. That's rarely the case. More often, they haven't been invited in a way that feels relevant, safe, or real.

So here's the charge. Audit your reach and expand your narrative. Because closing the inclusion gap isn't just the right thing to do, it's how real, resilient ecosystems get built.

Make Your Spaces More Welcoming

Innovation thrives where people feel like they belong. And yet, too many ecosystem spaces (i.e., coworking hubs, pitch nights, accelerator programs, etc.) end up feeling exclusive, even if unintentionally. It's not always about what's said or done explicitly. Sometimes, it's about what's missing: the invitation, the context, the signal that you belong here too.

We need to ask ourselves, who feels comfortable walking into our spaces, and who doesn't?

Let's start with the basics. Are we speaking a language the community understands? Startup culture loves jargon, "MVP," "Series A," "burn rate," but if someone's just trying to figure out how to turn their side hustle into a sustainable business, that language becomes a wall, not a bridge.

Design matters too. Look at your websites, flyers, and social media. Do the images reflect the diversity of your city? Do your materials explain things clearly, or do they assume insider knowledge? Plain language and inclusive visuals go a long way toward reducing friction.

But beyond aesthetics, think about where you're showing up. If every event is downtown at a tech-focused coworking space, don't be surprised if the same crowd keeps showing up. Try hosting events at libraries, barbershops, churches, community centers, or even public parks. Go where people already feel rooted.

And when people do show up, reduce the practical barriers. If possible, offer child care, transportation support, or just a meal. These small gestures communicate respect for people's time and circumstances.

Finally, enlist community ambassadors. These are trusted locals who can greet newcomers, answer questions, and help others feel at ease. You can't fake authenticity, but you can design for belonging. If someone walks into your space and thinks, "People like me don't belong here," then all the programs in the world won't matter.

Welcoming isn't a buzzword. It's the foundation for what you're trying to build.

Leverage Everyday Institutions

If you want to build a truly inclusive startup ecosystem, you can't sit back and wait for people to find you. Because as passionate as people are about their business or side hustle, not everyone sees themselves as "entrepreneurs," and not everyone feels invited into spaces labeled as "innovation hubs."

So instead of asking the community to come to you, flip the model. Bring the ecosystem to them.

That begins with partnering with the trusted institutions already embedded in people's daily lives. I'm talking about high schools, libraries, churches, barber shops, community centers, any place where people feel at home and not judged or that they don't belong.

Start with education partners. Local high schools and colleges are fertile ground for entrepreneurial mindsets; you just have to water the soil. Collaborate on creating entrepreneurship clubs, dual-enrollment courses, or job shadowing programs that connect students to real-world startup activity. When students see local models of success, they begin to imagine their own.

Then look at your public infrastructure. Libraries are more than places to borrow books. They're quiet, safe, accessible spaces. Use them for business basics workshops, one-on-one mentorship hours, or even temporary coworking pop-ups. Equip people with the tools to learn, build, and connect with your ecosystem.

Faith-based organizations are another powerful ally. Whether you're in a rural town or a mid-sized city, the church, mosque, or synagogue is often the most trusted community anchor. Sometimes the best innovators are sitting quietly in the pews. Work with these institutions to host financial literacy nights, small business expos, or storytelling sessions that celebrate everyday entrepreneurship.

Engage neighborhood associations to surface local needs and ideas. Host idea labs in rec centers or community halls. Listen first, then build programs that reflect what you hear.

And don't forget local media, the radio station, community newspapers, and social media groups. The social influencer that is always looking for content. Share the stories of real people doing real things. Celebrate the barber who launched his own product line or the grandmother selling cheese straws out of her home. These stories are powerful. They create resonance.

At the end of the day, you're not just building a startup ecosystem; you're weaving entrepreneurship into the cultural fabric of your city. That means showing up in the places where trust already lives. Because innovation doesn't just belong in glass buildings and pitch rooms. It belongs wherever people believe they can create something better.

Hunter of Wood—Real World Example

I first met Hunter when he was still a college student. Even then, there was something different about him. He wasn't just looking for a degree; he was looking for a new opportunity. His dad owns a cabinetry business, and he somehow knew that he too would become an entrepreneur.

Hunter grew up with a respect for the craft of woodworking and a curiosity for how old practices could be refined with new thinking. Hunter got some early wins. He won a popup competition from an area developer to give him free use of a space in the mall for the holiday season. He used this opportunity to launch a business that made custom wooden decorative household items. He joined the college makerspace to gain access to the tools he would need to build his product and the incubator for the tools he would need to build his company.

Over time, Hunter's company, Borowood, went from creating intricately designed household items that Hunter thought people might buy to building simple, fast turnaround, easy-to-ship products that customers actually wanted. Hunter tapped into the resources around him. He worked alongside advisers who helped refine his production process, developed his brand on social media, and connected with the broader manufacturing ecosystem.

Today, Borowood isn't just a business. It's a reminder that great ideas can come from anywhere and that with the right support, they can grow in places others might overlook. For Statesboro, Georgia, Hunter's journey is proof of what the ecosystem strives to do every day: equip entrepreneurs not just to dream, but to build. And in that way, Borowood is as much a part of the ecosystem's story as it is Hunter's.

Turn Community Members Into Ecosystem Allies

Startup ecosystems aren't just built by founders, funders, and facilitators; they're shaped and sustained by the broader community. And the most resilient ecosystems are the ones where everyone sees themselves as helping shape the local innovation story. That starts by shifting how we view community members: not as spectators, but as active contributors and co-creators of the entrepreneurial landscape.

Think about the people who already care deeply about your city. The small business owner who's kept their shop running for 20 years. The retired professional with decades of insight. The high schooler who's designing logos on Instagram. The pastor who counsels dozens of families a week. These aren't peripheral players; they're potential ecosystem allies. Your job is to give them meaningful ways to plug in.

Bring in a local chef to cater your next pitch night, not just for food, but to share their startup journey. That story might inspire someone else in the room to take their first leap. Invite retired accountants, lawyers, or business owners to hold office hours. They don't want full-time work, but they often want to give back.

Put youth groups to work designing flyers, videos, or social media content for entrepreneurship events. They'll learn valuable skills and see themselves as part of something bigger. That's community-building and capacity-building in one.

Don't just fill your advisory boards with suits. Add neighborhood leaders, teachers, or local artists to your board. These are the people who bring lived experience, street-level insight, and built-in trust.

And when it's time to run a pitch competition, think beyond just investors for your judging panel. Recruit a local barber, a principal, or a pastor. They know what matters in your community, and their presence signals that innovation belongs to everyone.

Because in the end, if your startup ecosystem only includes people with tech degrees or venture capital, it won't last. But if it includes people who know the city, love the city, and are ready to help shape its future, you're building something much stronger.

This isn't charity. It's strategy.

When people help build something, they fight harder to protect and sustain it. That's how movements grow. That's how ecosystems endure.

Action Checklist: Engaging the Broader Community

If we're serious about building startup ecosystems that actually reflect our communities and not just a select few individuals, we have to move beyond the usual suspects. This isn't about creating innovation for a handful of well-connected founders. It's about building something more equitable, more durable, and with more appeal. And that starts by intentionally engaging the full community.

Here's how you begin.

Start with a Participation Map—Not a Guess

Before you host another event or launch another program, stop and ask: Who's in the room and who isn't? Pull real data from your RSVPs, mentor rosters, and advisory boards. Then cross-reference it with your city's actual demographics. Chances are, there's a gap. That's your starting point. Don't think of it as a failure, just as a red flag.

Design with Inclusion, Not Just Intention

Whether it's a website, a flyer, or a physical space, make sure your design choices send a message of belonging. Use plain language. Avoid buzzwords. Represent a range of entrepreneurs in your visuals and not just the tech elite. If your community doesn't see themselves reflected, don't be surprised when they don't show up.

Bring the Work to Everyday Spaces

We don't need another hotel ballroom or boardroom meetup. We need more events in barber shops, libraries, churches, and high school cafeterias. All the places where trust already exists. When you show up in people's daily lives, you signal that this work is for them too.

Partner with Institutions People Already Trust

Some of your most powerful ecosystem allies are your least flashy: the librarian who's been mentoring teens for years, the teacher running an after-school business club, the neighborhood pastor who sees untapped hustle every day. Don't ask them to attend your ecosystem. Invite them to shape it.

Make Engagement Easy and Real

If the only way to contribute is to lead a committee, we've already lost. Give people meaningful, bite-sized ways to plug into your ecosystem. Ask them to judge a pitch night, design a flyer, or offer one hour of mentorship. The goal is to create momentum, not bureaucracy.

Tell Better, Broader Stories

If the only success story you're sharing is a tech founder who raised venture capital, your messaging is missing the mark. Place a spotlight on the single mom that's launching a home-based catering business.

The retired mechanic that's mentoring student inventors. The side-hustler that's building something real after their shift ends. These are the faces of entrepreneurship too, and they deserve the mic.

Measure What Matters

Don't just track how many people came. Track who came. Did your event draw in folks from outside downtown? Did you see more women, more students, or more people of color? If not, adjust. Inclusion is a metric, not a tagline.

If your ecosystem only feels relevant to the already-plugged-in, it won't last. Real innovation takes root when everyone feels like they have a stake in the outcome and a seat at the table. This isn't about charity. It's about building the kind of community where more people believe they can build. Because once they believe, they do. And when they do, everything changes.

Make It Belong to Everyone

If there's one thing I've learned from years of working in smaller markets and overlooked communities, it's that ecosystems that last are ecosystems that belong.

Not just to the mayor's office.

Not just to the local university.

Not just to the founders who already know the handshake and the shorthand.

But to everyone.

The barber who knows more about community trust than any consultant ever could.

The high school student soliciting community-wide support to make and donate blankets for foster kids.

The retired Air Force veteran mentoring a first-time founder.

The immigrant mother starting a food business to support her family.

We have to stop building startup ecosystems that are more exclusive, curated, insider-driven and start treating them like shared spaces of possibility where anyone with an idea and a spark of ambition feels like they have a shot. Less cliquey. More inclusive.

That kind of belonging doesn't happen by accident. It happens when we:

- Listen to people who don't usually get asked.

- Design intentionally for accessibility, not just for aesthetics.

- Invite a broad selection of players, and not just to attend, but to contribute.

- As the work changes, share credit, ownership, and leadership.

People show up when they feel like they matter. They give when they feel heard. And when they feel ownership, they protect and sustain what's been built long after the first grant ends or the founding team moves on.

If we do this right, we won't just create ecosystems that launch startups. We'll create ecosystems that uplift cities. Places where the idea of owning your own business becomes more than an economic strategy. It becomes a cultural expectation.

We'll send a signal that this is a place where everyone can build, belong, and believe.

That's the kind of legacy you should leave.

Chapter 10: Building for the Long Haul

We've come a long way on our adventure thus far. We've explored how to assess your community's readiness, how to pull together stewards, and what type of programs to offer and where to offer them. We've highlighted the importance of funding your ecosystem and capturing your metrics. But now, the real test begins—the question that determines whether the work we've done will truly matter in the long run. Can it endure?

Not for a season. Not until the grant runs dry or the headlines fade. But for generations. Can your ecosystem become the kind of civic infrastructure that lives beyond the founders and outlasts any one institution's commitment? Can it still be creating opportunity, solving problems, and sparking innovation when no one remembers who hosted the first pitch night or launched the original accelerator?

Because that's the goal. That's the game we should be playing. It's not about press releases, ribbon cuttings, or plaques on a building. It's about building an ecosystem with deep enough roots to weather inevitable storms and strong enough branches to support new growth we haven't even imagined yet.

Too often, startup initiatives are built like pop-up shops. There's lots of excitement at the outset, but over time that excitement wanes. What we need instead are economic engines that are embedded in the fabric of our communities. That kind of permanence doesn't happen by accident. It requires intention. It requires alignment. And it requires time.

In this chapter, we're going to talk about what it takes to play the long game. We'll unpack the systems that foster resilience, the decisions that future-proof our efforts, and the cultural commitments that make people feel like the ecosystem belongs to them. We'll do this because only an ecosystem that belongs to everyone can truly last.

Start With the End in Mind

When you set out to build a startup ecosystem, it's easy to get caught up in the excitement of the ribbon cuttings, the pitch competitions, and the Instagrammable coworking spaces. But if you want your ecosystem to matter when the picture op is finished, you need to change your attitude from starting something new to making something that will last.

To achieve this, I want you to think of your ecosystem like a tree. Initially, it's a sapling. It's delicate, tentative, and reliant on outside support. It needs nurturing. It needs to be protected. And like a young tree, it can have trouble getting a grip on the ground or bending when it gets too much pressure. But if you give it the correct amount of care, time, and the right conditions, it will start to grow roots. In your ecosystem, those roots connect to the community. They reach into schools, local governments, economic development agencies, and the culture itself.

Over time, your ecosystem matures. It becomes self-sustaining. It can handle changes in leadership, the economy, and politics. It becomes a location where not just firms start up, but also where founders come back to help others, young people can see themselves as entrepreneurs, and the whole community is proud of the innovation that is happening right in their own backyard.

But that kind of generational impact doesn't happen by default. It happens by design. That's why you have to ask yourself early:

What will this look like in ten years?

Who will own it?

Who will lead it?

How will it evolve when you're no longer in the room?

If you don't have clear, honest answers to those questions, then you're not building an ecosystem. You're building a moment. And moments fade.

Longevity requires foresight. It requires humility. And above all, it requires that we think beyond our own tenure, our own institutions, and even our own intentions. The most durable ecosystems are the ones designed to outgrow their original architects.

So before you plant another flag or schedule another launch event, take the time to map the endgame. Because the decisions you make today will shape whether this ecosystem is still standing strong a decade from now or whether it withers when the first storm rolls through.

Build Institutions, Not Just Events

It's easy to get swept up in the energy of the event cycle. A startup weekend draws a crowd. An accelerator cohort gets press. A grant-funded pilot makes funders feel good. And all of these things can be valuable and make you feel excited, at least for a while. But if that's all you're building, you're not building a startup ecosystem. You're building a series of pop-up experiences. And when the funding ends or the champion leaves, so does the momentum.

If we're serious about long-term impact, we need to focus less on creating excitement and more on building infrastructure. I'm not talking about infrastructure in the form of roads and fiber optics, although those are important, but in the form of institutions. Anchors. The things that people can rely on.

Your goal should be to build anchor institutions that:

- Provide consistent, predictable support for entrepreneurs so that a first-time founder knows where to go for help, today or five years from now;

- Outlast individual champions, grant cycles, or political administrations, because if one person's departure brings the whole thing down, it was never stable to begin with;

- Earn trust by being deeply embedded and woven into the local culture, economy, and identity of the community and not perched above it.

These institutions don't always have to be formal. Yes, innovation hubs, incubators, and nonprofit intermediaries matter. But so do the informal networks of founder peer groups, mentorship circles, community Slack channels, and meetup groups that are consistent and collaborative.

The key is that these structures are organized, resourced, and accountable. They have a purpose beyond the hype, a plan beyond the pilot, and a presence that can be counted on.

Yes, flashy launches get attention. But it's the boring, durable stuff, like the governance models, the partnerships, the operating budgets, and the succession planning, that makes ecosystems stick.

Keep in mind that events make noise. Institutions make change. If you want your startup city to thrive long after you've moved on, don't just throw parties. Build permanence.

Design for Leadership Transitions

If there's one failure point I see time and again in growing ecosystems, it's this: What happens when the champion leaves?

It's easy to build momentum when you have a passionate leader. Someone who hustles, connects, inspires, and makes things happen through sheer force of will. But ecosystems that rely on singular heroes are fragile by design. The departure of a charismatic founder, a visionary program director, or a well-connected public servant shouldn't bring your ecosystem to a halt. And yet, in too many communities it does. What you need are systems, not saviors.

It is through this realization that real ecosystem maturity begins. It's when you stop optimizing for the present leader and start designing for the future. That means building structures that make leadership transitions expected and not something that jeopardizes the stability of the ecosystem. It means understanding that the mark of a healthy ecosystem isn't just what happens while you're leading it but what continues after you're gone.

If you want to make sure your work lasts:

- Make a shared record of all the programs, relationships, and processes. Don't let important historical information stay in someone's thoughts or email.

- Create a diverse advisory or governing board that can keep things going, help guide the vision, and make sure the ecosystem is doing what it should.

- Make succession plans for who will take over important jobs as they become available. This is especially critical for jobs that connect different stakeholder groups.

- Change the leaders of working groups and task forces every so often to share expertise, keep people from getting burned out, and build a bigger pool of experienced contributors.

- Find and train new leaders, especially those from groups that aren't well represented, so that your ecosystem shows the whole potential of your community, not just those who already have access.

You want to promote change and make it clear that leadership changes should be welcomed and even applauded. These things mean growth, not failure.

If your ecosystem is only as strong as its current leader, then it's not really an ecosystem. It's more of a personality project. True startup ecosystems aren't built on individuals. They're built on shared values, distributed leadership, and resilient structures.

So plan for the handoff. Bake succession into your design from day one. Because the most powerful thing a leader can do isn't just to lead well; it's to prepare others to lead even better.

Diversify and Normalize Funding

We touched on this back in Chapter 7, but it's worth revisiting because nothing undermines a promising ecosystem faster than financial instability. Stability doesn't just come from passion. It comes from predictability. And in ecosystems, predictability is spelled f-u-n-d-i-n-g.

All too often, early-stage efforts are built on a patchwork of one-time grants, short-term sponsorships, and hopeful crowdfunding campaigns. That might get you through the launch, maybe even a cohort or two, but it won't get you through the next decade. If your programs live or die by every grant cycle, then your ecosystem isn't really operating; it's merely surviving. And survival mode doesn't leave much room for vision, growth, or purposeful community engagement.

So let's talk about what financial maturity looks like.

As you are building out your ecosystem, work toward establishing:

- Multi-year funding commitments from anchor institutions, such as universities, local governments, chambers, or philanthropic foundations that believe in your long-term impact;

- Earned revenue streams; whether it's coworking space rentals, entrepreneurship trainings, memberships, or hosted events, if people find value in what you're offering, let them pay for it;

- Recurring budget lines from city, county, or regional agencies; unlike one-time grants, these would be institutional support that's written into annual budgets and reflect a shared stake in your success;

- A clear funding roadmap that aligns with your 5- or 10-year vision, so you're not just chasing money; you're attracting partners who share your purpose.

The goal is to normalize funding. It is to make it part of the operational rhythm and not something that you're constantly chasing. That takes discipline, planning, and relationship-building. But it also sends a powerful signal: We're not a flash in the pan. We're part of the civic infrastructure now.

As you gain momentum and maturity, the money will follow. When funders see that you've moved beyond the startup phase and built a stable foundation, they're more likely to commit. You'll find that longevity inspires confidence.

So don't treat funding as a one-off pursuit. Make it part of your design. Because if you want your ecosystem to thrive for years and not just survive the next quarter, it needs financial legs strong enough to carry the vision forward.

Embed in Policy and Planning

If you want your ecosystem to last, it can't just exist in the business community's imagination. It needs to be part of the city's DNA. In small cities especially, longevity is earned when entrepreneurial support becomes a public priority and not just a private sector project.

Too many startup ecosystems operate in isolation. They run parallel to the real work of city-building rather than as an integral part of it. And while that might work for a while, it's not how you build staying power. If your ecosystem is seen as an add-on, or worse, a luxury, then it becomes one of the first things to get cut when priorities shift or budgets tighten.

The alternative? Make entrepreneurship part of the civic infrastructure.

This means that you need to be:

- Incorporating entrepreneurship into city and regional economic development plans, and not just as a footnote but as a core strategy for job creation, talent retention, and economic mobility;

- Aligning your efforts with workforce strategies, zoning ordinances, and educational pipelines to ensure that startups are growing not in spite of local policy, but because of it;

- Building consistent relationships with elected officials, economic development leaders, and city staff, and not just during grant season or when you need a budget line, but year-round, as collaborative partners in community development.

When startup growth is seen as a public good, as something essential to a city's health and resilience, then it gains more than attention. It gains legitimacy. It becomes a protected part of the civic agenda. And that's how ecosystems survive leadership turnover, economic downturns, and shifting political winds.

Embedding in policy doesn't mean compromising your agility. It means securing your relevance. If you want your work to endure beyond your tenure, then you need to plant it not just in the market but also in the municipality. Because when the city incorporates entrepreneurship into its blueprint, it not only supports it but also sustains it.

Leave Room for Evolution

If the goal is to build something that lasts, that doesn't mean you lock it in place and hope the world doesn't change around you. Because it will. The startups in your ecosystem will pivot. Markets will shift. Technology will leap ahead. The funding climate will tighten or loosen. Community needs will change and evolve, sometimes rapidly. If your ecosystem isn't built to evolve with them, then you're not building for endurance. You're building for obsolescence.

Resilience isn't about staying the same; it's about adapting with purpose. To stay relevant over time, you need to build in mechanisms for reflection, correction, and reinvention. That means:

- Holding an annual strategy review session with ecosystem partners. Not just to check boxes, but to ask real questions: What's working? What's changed? Where do we need to grow?

- Sunsetting outdated programs that no longer meet a clear need. Don't feel as though you have to let things linger. It's okay to retire what's run its course and to pivot to something that will resonate with the current crop of founders.

- Piloting small experiments, such as new formats, partnerships, technologies, or delivery models that allow you to test and learn without overcommitting resources.

- Keeping channels for feedback from founders, funders, educators, and the broader community open so that you stay grounded in reality and not just on the strategy decks.

The ecosystems that endure aren't the ones that try to freeze time. They're the ones that know how to hold their purpose steady while letting their methods adapt.

A thriving ecosystem is a learning ecosystem. It treats every program, policy, and partner as a living asset. Something that can grow, shift, or even be replaced as conditions demand. It knows that agility isn't the enemy of stability, but rather it's the engine of it.

I've lived through several hurricanes in different parts of the country. And I can tell you that different trees handle the sheer force of the wind differently. I'm sure you've seen them on TV. A Category 4 storm hits the Florida coast, and you see sabal palms thrashing in the wind, bending wildly but not breaking. Then a similar-strength storm rolls through the South. And there lay pine tree after pine tree. Either uprooted or snapped in half by the wind.

When it comes to your ecosystem, build with flexibility in mind. Don't build something so rigid that it cracks under pressure or under the winds of change. Build something like a sabal palm, where its flexibility can withstand the strongest of winds and its deep roots keep you grounded. Build something so responsive to the needs of your founders that it remains essential, no matter what the future holds. That's how you ensure that your ecosystem doesn't just survive the next decade but leads it.

Action Checklist: Building for the Long Haul

We've outlined the core components of a lasting startup ecosystem. We've discussed its vision, structure, funding, leadership, and adaptability. But none of that matters unless you turn those principles into action. The ecosystems that last are not the ones with the best slogans. They are the ones with a sound plan and the ability to take action.

This is how to turn your momentum into a strong, long-lasting infrastructure:

Set a 5- and 10-Year Vision with Your Partners

Don't make your plan by yourself. Get together with your most important stakeholders, such as colleges, city leaders, business owners, and investors, and come up with a long-term vision that everyone can agree on. Where do you want this ecosystem to be in a decade? What kind of impact should it have? Use that vision to guide your decisions, prioritize investments, and hold each other accountable over time.

Transition Programs into Formal Institutions or Embedded Roles

Great events are a good start, but they need a place to stay. Make your one-time projects into permanent programs, staffed roles, or

250|

physical venues that are part of established institutions. Whether it's a university-backed center, a city-funded position, or a nonprofit intermediary, give your efforts roots that can grow.

Document Systems and Create Leadership Continuity Plans

Don't let the memories be what keeps your ecosystem going. Put your procedures, relationships, and partnerships down on paper. Make plans for who will take over key roles when they become available. Set up ways for leaders to grow so that institutional knowledge is not lost when someone quits, changes jobs, or retires.

Diversify and Stabilize Funding Sources

Getting money shouldn't be a race every year. Get a balance of long-term commitments, earned income, and governmental help. Make your budget as strong as your vision. The more you can count on your resources, the more strategic your choices can be.

Align with Public Policy and Civic Planning

Don't just sit on the sidelines. Make sure that your job is part of the city's and the region's top priorities. Make your ecosystem a force for community vitality, job development, and economic growth that includes everyone. You can stay in power when you're part of the civic agenda.

Build Feedback Loops and Room for Continuous Evolution

Ecosystems that can learn and change are the strongest. They make sure that founders, partners, and community members can give them honest feedback on a frequent basis. So, always be curious. Pilot new ideas. Retire what no longer works. Flexibility isn't the opposite of stability; it's the foundation of it.

Remember that building for the long haul isn't about locking things in place. It's about creating the conditions for growth, adaptation, and shared ownership over time. Do these things, and your ecosystem won't just survive the next chapter; it'll be ready to write it.

Build Something You'd Be Proud to Hand Off

In the end, the real measure of your ecosystem's success isn't how much press it gets, how many startups it launches, or how many metrics you can pack into a year-end report. It's this: Would you be proud to hand it off? Because at some point, you will.

Whether you're leading from a university, city hall, the private sector, or a community nonprofit, your time in the driver's seat is temporary. The question is not whether you'll step aside. The question is what will you leave behind?

If your ecosystem collapses when you move on, then it was never truly a system. It was a project. And projects don't endure. But ecosystems, when done right, do. Not because they're flashy or flawless, but because they're embedded, co-owned, and continuously nurtured by many hands over time.

Your goal isn't to build the next Silicon Valley. And frankly, your city doesn't need that. What it needs and deserves is an ecosystem built with clarity of purpose, care for people, and commitment to place. A system where ideas don't just get pitched; they grow.

A place where young talent doesn't have to leave to chase their dreams. A culture where entrepreneurship isn't reserved for the well-connected but is a visible, viable path for anyone with the courage to try. And a local economy where possibility feels personal, not imported.

That is what legacy looks like. Not a logo. Not a launch event. But a community asset that is shared, resilient, and rooted.

So as you build, think ahead. Build something you'd be proud to hand off, because one day you will. And when you do, let the next generation inherit more than programs or partnerships. Let them inherit a belief in their place, in their potential, and in each other.

That's the real legacy of a startup city.

CHAPTER 11:
THE ROLE OF
STORYTELLING IN
ECOSYSTEM BUILDING

> *"The most powerful person in the world is the storyteller. The storyteller sets the vision, values and agenda of an entire generation that is to come."*
>
> -Steve Jobs, *co-founder, Apple Inc.*

In every small city that's starting to build an ecosystem, there's been a moment, usually early on, when someone leans in and asks a deceptively simple question, "What's our pitch?"

They're not talking about an investor deck or a tech startup's elevator spiel. What they mean is:

"What's our story? Why should anyone believe that our city could be a hub of innovation?"

And that question, while often asked with hesitation or skepticism, is the beginning of something very powerful. In the process of establishing startup ecosystems, storytelling serves as more than just a decorative element; it serves as a fundamental instrument.

It shapes how people perceive your city, both from the outside and from within. It gives funders a reason to write checks, partners a reason to say yes, and founders a reason to stay. It can open doors that metrics alone can't. And perhaps most importantly, it helps your community see itself as a place of potential, advancement, and possibility instead of as second-tier or "too small."

Branding isn't the only thing that marketing and storytelling are about. It's about feeling like you belong. They assist you in figuring out what your ecosystem is all about, who it's for, and where it's going. And when done correctly, they build up energy that spreadsheets can't show.

This chapter is about figuring out how stories fit into creating ecosystems. It's about discovering how to find your story, how to tell it authentically, and how to make it stick. We'll look at real examples of cities that shifted perception by shifting the story they told about themselves and what happened when their residents started to see innovation not as something that happens elsewhere, but as something that can happen here.

Because in the end, you can have the best strategy, the strongest partnerships, and the most polished programs, but if no one hears your story, you're building in silence.

Let's make sure your city gets heard.

Why Storytelling Matters

Most small cities aren't making headlines for billion-dollar exits or Fortune 500 expansions. And that's okay. Because impact doesn't have to come from scale. It can come from story.

I've worked in and with communities where the entrepreneurs don't wear hoodies and pitch to venture capitalists. They wear work boots, teach fourth grade, cut hair, or care for aging parents. They're students juggling side hustles. Veterans launching second careers. Parents solving problems that no one else noticed. These are the stories that really matter. Not because they're flashy, but because they're real. And they reflect the full, human face of innovation.

If you look hard enough, you'll see that your city is full of these stories. You just have to tell them. And you have to tell them loudly and often. Because in ecosystem building, storytelling isn't just about marketing. It's an amplifier of your community's story. When you shine a light on local founders and changemakers, you're not just reporting what happened; you're actively shaping the way your community sees itself. And that has ripple effects across everything you're trying to build.

The benefits of strong storytelling can be profound. Here are a few ways in which storytelling can positively impact your ecosystem:

- **Attract Capital:** Investors don't just back business plans; they back people. When you craft a compelling story, it gives your ecosystem a heart and makes the opportunity relatable. That narrative helps cut through the noise and build trust between your ecosystem and the people looking to invest in it.

- **Inspire Local Talent:** If people don't see someone like themselves starting a business, they may never view it as an option. Storytelling builds belief. It makes entrepreneurship feel local, not distant.

- **Earn Media Attention:** Reporters are drawn to stories that are personal and place-specific. We all know the story of Michael Dell. A good founder story doesn't just get local coverage; it can elevate your ecosystem and your city's brand far beyond the city limits.

- **Build Partnerships:** Stakeholders are more likely to invest time, money, or political capital when they feel a sense of emotional connection. Good stories help build that bridge.

- **Shape Identity:** Over time, the stories you tell define the culture of your ecosystem. They influence how your community thinks, what it values, and how it responds to change.

When you commit to telling your city's story and to doing it with honesty, consistency, and heart, you're doing more than documentation. You're defining your city's identity. You're setting the tone for what's possible and who gets to participate.

And in a world where perception often shapes reality, that's not a soft skill—it's a strategic one.

Tell Stories That Resonate

Too often, when people think about entrepreneurship stories, their minds go straight to unicorn valuations, elite accelerators, and founders who just happen to know a dozen venture capitalists. But that's not the narrative most small cities need. And it's certainly not the one that builds belief.

The most effective ecosystem stories—the ones that actually move people—aren't about perfection. They're about progress. About grit. About transformation. They show how entrepreneurship happens in real life, under real constraints, with real stakes—and that's what makes them powerful.

Here's what you should be looking to highlight:

- The immigrant entrepreneur who started a catering business out of her kitchen, building a client base dish by dish, eventually hiring her neighbors and reinvesting in her community.

- The teenager who taught himself to code and built a hyperlocal app to help residents navigate bus routes or report potholes—because no one else had.

- The barber in the area who opened a second shop, hired young people, and made his business a place where kids from rough backgrounds could learn from him.

- The retired nurse who identified a need for wellness aftercare and started a coaching business to help others live healthier, more fulfilling lives.

- The family-run bakery that almost went out of business during COVID but swiftly switched to online orders, home delivery, and virtual baking classes and kept all of its employees.

These aren't outliers. They're proof points. They demonstrate that entrepreneurship isn't just for tech bros in urban high-rises.

It's for everyone—teachers, tradespeople, teenagers, and retirees. It's not about who you know. It's about what you build.

And when you tell these stories—consistently, proudly, and through the voices of those living them—you create a shift. People stop seeing entrepreneurship as something that happens "out there" and start seeing it as something that can happen right here. They begin to see themselves in the story. And when that happens, a quiet question begins to rise:

"Why not me?"

That's the spark that every ecosystem needs. Not just awareness. Not just interest. But belief. And belief is born when the stories you tell don't just inform—they resonate.

Make Founders the Face of the Ecosystem

One of the most common mistakes I see in small-city ecosystem building is this: institutions, not individuals, tell the story.

You'll see press releases about new grants, ribbon cuttings at coworking spaces, or logos from universities and agencies splashed across every event banner. And while those institutions play a critical role—make no mistake—the heart of your ecosystem isn't your buildings, your programs, or your org chart.

It's your founders.

If you want to build a brand people rally around, make the entrepreneurs your heroes. Let them—not the institutions that support them—be the face of your narrative. Because when people connect with a founder's journey, they see a human story, not a business one. And that's what encourages belonging, builds pride, and fuels momentum.

Here are some simple but powerful ways to highlight your founders:

- Feature some Q&As from founders on your website or social media. Ask them about their first sale, their biggest challenge, and what they love about being an entrepreneur in your city. Keep it authentic and unfiltered.

- Use short quotes or video clips at public events. Let their words and voices ground your message. Don't just talk about entrepreneurship; show it in motion.

- Invite founders to speak on panels, join boards, and help shape programming. They shouldn't just attend events; they should help lead them. Let them shape the ecosystem they're part of.

- Partner with local media to run a recurring "Founder Friday" series, which could be a column or short feature that puts the spotlight on a different entrepreneur each week. Over time, this becomes a drumbeat of local innovation.

- Tell the full origin stories. Go deeper than just what the product is or how the company started. Share how the idea came to be. Talk about the sleepless nights, the risks they took, the career opportunities they left behind, the setbacks they experienced, and the personal sacrifices. These are the narratives that make startups in your city relatable.

When you let founders lead the storytelling, you do more than elevate their profiles; you place a face to your ecosystem and humanize it. You turn the abstract idea of entrepreneurship into lived experiences, and you build pride not in an institution, but in people. And that gives your city a human brand—one people want to support, invest in, and belong to.

Because at the end of the day, it's not the grant awards or organizational charts that inspire others to act. It's stories about people who tried, struggled, and still showed up.

Let the founders speak. Let their stories shine. That's how you make your ecosystem real and that's how you make it theirs.

Control the Narrative—Before Others Do

If you're not actively working with the founders to shape the narrative about your local innovation ecosystem, someone else will. And more often than not, they'll get it wrong. They'll lean on tired stereotypes, outdated assumptions, and secondhand impressions. And once those take root, they're hard to dislodge.

You've probably heard the usual refrains:

"There's no real innovation happening here."

"Small cities don't have the talent."

"Everyone leaves after college anyway."

"It's just a good ol' boys club."

These aren't just harmless comments. They're subtle, corrosive messages that shape how funders, policymakers, and even residents see your city. If you leave them unchecked, they chip away at the confidence, credibility, and momentum that you're trying to build.

But there's some good news. You can replace those messages, those myths, with better stories. More truthful stories about how your ecosystem is growing. Stories that are rooted in progress, in people, in the hard work, and in the real wins that are occurring right now, not someday.

And that means that telling stories should be a key component of your strategy, not just something you do when you have time.

Here are a few easy things you can do to get your story back:

- Write down every win you have, no matter how big or small. Every step forward is important. A founder's first hire. A new partnership. A startup making its first export. These are signals of momentum.

- Celebrate progress and not just perfection. You don't need billion-dollar exits to tell a good story. Show the messy middle. The grind. The resilience. That's where people connect.

- Repeat your ecosystem's values as early and as often as you can. If you want to be known for being inclusive, accessible, or founder-led, say it. Say it in your events, your signage, your social media—everywhere. Repetition builds recognition.

- Track your milestones publicly. A timeline of progress reminds people that things are moving. Keep a record. Chronicle the evolution. Make it visible.

Because perception isn't shaped by facts alone; it's shaped by repetition. If people keep hearing that your city is a place where ideas thrive, where founders are supported, and where innovation is local—not imported—they'll start to believe it. And when they believe it, they act differently. They invest differently. They stay.

So don't let the old myths win by default. Take control of the story. Own it. Tell it often. And make sure the story your city is known for is one your community is proud to live by.

Use Storytelling as a Strategic Tool

Too often, storytelling in small-city ecosystems is treated as an afterthought. It's something someone gets around to when the grant report is due or when a new website goes live. But if we're serious about building ecosystems that attract capital, retain talent, and create a sense of shared purpose, then storytelling can't be reactive or accidental. It needs to be intentional. Embedded. Strategic.

Think of storytelling not as a side activity but as a tool that is just as critical to your ecosystem as your CRM, your programming calendar, or your budget spreadsheet. Why? Because storytelling doesn't just describe what's happening. It gives meaning to the work. It translates data into emotion and emotion into action.

Here's how you can, and should, be using stories across your ecosystem strategy:

- **Pitch Funders:** Don't just talk about outputs. Share the human side of your impact. Instead of "we hosted three workshops," tell the story of a founder who got their first investor meeting because of one of those workshops. Frame your *need* through real-world *change*.

- **Rally Partners:** Partners can get fatigued. Stories reenergize. Remind collaborators why this work matters and who it's for, what's at stake, and how their support translates into real transformation.

- **Engage Policymakers:** Numbers are important, but narratives make an impression that sticks. Show elected officials how entrepreneurship is improving the lives in their own districts. Make it personal. Make it local.

- **Educate the Public:** Normalize risk, celebrate resilience, and help your community understand that failure isn't the end of a journey; it's just a part of the process. Storytelling can demystify entrepreneurship and make it more approachable.

- **Attract Talent:** Give people a reason to root for your city. If a designer in Atlanta or a developer in Chicago hears a compelling story about one of your founders and your community's grit, then they might just start thinking: Maybe there's a place for me there too.

To do this well, consider building a **story bank**—a curated collection of founder profiles, quotes, testimonials, program milestones, and media features. Think of it as your ecosystem's narrative toolbox. When you need a quick anecdote for a speech, a powerful example for a proposal, or a spotlight story for a newsletter—you'll have it ready. It can be used in reports to funders to enhance the metrics.

Strategic storytelling isn't about spin. It's about substance. It's about capturing what's real and sharing it in a way that moves people from curious observer to committed partner. From passive resident to active participant.

So start telling your stories proudly, consistently, and with purpose. Because every ecosystem is made of people. And people are moved by stories.

Action Checklist: Embedding Storytelling in Your Ecosystem

If you want storytelling to drive your ecosystem forward, you can't treat it as a side project. It needs to be part of the culture. Part of the rhythm. Something everyone sees as core to the mission—not just the marketing.

Storytelling isn't fluff. It's a force multiplier. It amplifies your wins, personalizes your data, and reminds your community who and what you're building for.

And like anything else in your ecosystem—capital, partnerships, talent—it needs infrastructure and intention to truly scale.

Here's how to embed storytelling as a strategic strength:

- Identify a diverse range of founders to profile regularly

  Make sure your stories reflect the full spectrum of your community—across race, gender, age, industry, and lived experience. When people see themselves in your ecosystem, they're more likely to join it.

- Have founders be the public face of events, activities, and relationships.

  Don't just speak about starting a business; show it. Let founders open events, co-design initiatives, and speak on behalf of your ecosystem. This builds authenticity and human connection.

- Teach team members or community allies how to share stories and gather information.

You don't need a full media team. Show your staff, interns, or ecosystem advocates how to interview founders, get testimonies, and make short videos or social media posts. The stories are already happening; give people the tools they need to see and share them.

- Work with local media, freelancers, or students to tell and share stories.

  Journalism classes, AV clubs in high school, or freelance writers can all be very helpful. Give them a platform, a purpose, and a pipeline of stories, and let them help you scale your narrative reach.

- Don't just count participants; tell their stories. Use story-based metrics in reporting to describe who was impacted, how they were impacted, and why it matters. Funders and stakeholders want to understand the human impact that your ecosystem is having. A single story can be more persuasive than a spreadsheet or list of metrics.

- Keep your story bank current. Update it quarterly with new wins and profiles.

- Keep a centralized folder with founder bios, quotes, case studies, photos, and milestones. Organize it by industry, program, or audience so that it's accessible and easy to reference when you need it.

- Repeat your ecosystem's purpose, values, and identity often. Every time you share a story, you reinforce what your ecosystem stands for. This repetition doesn't just inform the community; it shapes its culture. Over time,

> it defines what people expect, what they celebrate, and what they support.

Great ecosystems don't just launch businesses—they build belief. And belief is fueled by story. Make it a habit. Make it a strategy. Make it part of how your community understands what's possible. Because when people hear the right stories often enough, they stop asking "Can this happen here?" and start saying, "It already is."

Stories Build Movements

Let's be clear: metrics matter. They help validate progress, justify funding, and chart a course forward. But numbers alone don't build belief. They don't stir emotion or inspire action. People don't follow metrics—they follow meaning.

In small cities especially, the story you tell about who you are—and who you could be—can shape everything. It influences whether a student decides to stay and build, whether a parent sees entrepreneurship as an option for their child, and whether a local policymaker sees innovation as a priority worth protecting.

At its core, storytelling is about helping people answer four simple, powerful questions:

- What kind of place do I live in?

- What's possible here?

- What are people like me accomplishing?

- And is it worth trying?

When you highlight local founders who are taking chances and making change and tell their stories of grit, creativity, and progress, you begin to rewrite the collective imagination of your city. You bring entrepreneurship from a theoretical realm that lives in classrooms, TV shows, and pipedreams into the everyday lives of the people around you. And when your community begins to see itself not just as a place where businesses open, but as a place where ideas thrive and people grow, the vibe in your city begins to shift. Entrepreneurship becomes not just viable but visible. Not just relevant but reachable.

So here's the charge:

Tell your stories. Loudly. Frequently. Authentically.

Don't wait for the perfect headline. Don't wait for someone else to do it. Start with what you have. Lift up the voices already in your ecosystem. Celebrate the journey, not just the destination.

Because the more you reinforce the idea that this is a city where innovation belongs, the more likely it is to become true. Not by accident. But by belief—amplified and shared through story.

Stories don't just inform.

They connect.

They inspire.

They build movements.

Conclusion: This Is Where the Work Begins

> *"The journey of a thousand miles begins with a single step."*
>
> -Lao Tzu, *Chinese philosopher*

By now, we've gone over the most important parts of creating a successful startup ecosystem in a small city. We've changed the meaning of "ecosystem" from a group of programs to a network of living interactions. We've talked about how to get the proper people involved, how to establish infrastructure that will last, and how to help entrepreneurs with programs and systems. We've talked about how important it is to get money from different sources, to establish a culture on purpose, to measure what really counts, and to tell the story of your city with honesty and pride.

But if there's one thing I want you to remember, it's that developing a startup environment is not a list of things to do.

You are making a promise to your house, your neighbors, and individuals you will never meet.

It's not about launching an incubator or accelerator just because another city did. It's not about hosting a demo day, winning a grant, or checking boxes to satisfy funders. Those things might generate attention, but attention fades. Commitment doesn't.

This work—the real work—is about consistency. It's about resilience. It's about showing up year after year to build trust with founders who've never had a seat at the table. It's about creating opportunities in places where opportunity once felt distant. It's about stitching together belief across institutions, across neighborhoods, and across generations.

And perhaps most importantly, it's about redefining what's possible in places that have too often been told that innovation belongs elsewhere. That startups happen on the coasts. That big ideas don't come from small towns. That entrepreneurship is for someone else.

You are here to question that story. You're here to show that your city has the talent, creativity, determination, and vision to make something big, meaningful, and long-lasting. So don't think of this book as a blueprint to finish. Think of it as a starting point for the commitment ahead. The ecosystem you are creating involves more than just launching businesses; it is fundamentally about instilling belief. And belief, once rooted, can change everything.

You're Not Just Building Startups—You're Building Capacity

Of course, launching startups is a goal. But it's not **the** goal.

If you're doing this work right, what you're really building isn't just a pipeline of pitch-ready ventures. You're building capacity. Human capacity. Civic capacity. The kind of capacity that strengthens a city from the inside out.

Because the best ecosystems don't just produce companies that scale. They produce communities that believe. That collaborate. That grow stronger over time.

What does that look like in practice? Well, it looks like

- **Creating on-ramps for first-time founders.** Founders such as the teacher with a side hustle, the barber with a business idea, and the retired mechanic with a patent sketch in his garage. You're not waiting for "investor-ready" startups. You're meeting people where they are and helping them move forward.

- **Retaining talent that might otherwise leave.** Whether it's the local college grad, the mid-career professional, or the teenager with a big idea, your ecosystem gives people a reason to stay and a pathway to contribute.

- **Encouraging risk-taking in communities that have learned to play it safe.** In many small cities, failure isn't just feared; it's stigmatized. Your work builds a culture where trying something new is not only accepted but also celebrated.

- **Rebuilding trust in institutions through transparency and shared ownership.** When city agencies, universities, and support organizations open their doors and co-create with founders, something powerful happens: credibility is restored.

- **Connecting people across lines of race, class, and sector.** Entrepreneurship becomes a bridge between neighborhoods, generations, and industries that rarely sit at the same table.

- **Turning local problems into local opportunities.** Whether it's access to healthy food, childcare, broadband, or small-scale manufacturing, your ecosystem helps residents become problem solvers, not just recipients of someone else's solution.

That's the deeper work. That's the long game. That's the kind of capacity that doesn't just produce startups; it produces a stronger, more resilient city.

So don't sell your efforts short by measuring them only in exits or funding rounds.

You are building belief. You are building belonging. You are building the infrastructure of possibility.

And that's the work worth doing.

Every City Has Seeds. Some Just Need Cultivating

It really doesn't matter if you live in the rural South, the industrial Midwest, or at the foot of the Rocky Mountains; every city has potential.

Every city has talent.

Every city has seeds.

Some just need cultivating.

Over the course of writing this book and walking alongside dozens of communities on their startup journey, I've seen the same story unfold in the most unlikely of places. Not in Silicon Valley. Not in a tech corridor. But in small towns with shuttered factories, mid-sized cities with downtowns struggling to find their next identity, and rural regions where "entrepreneur" once felt like a foreign word.

And yet, in all those places, the spark was the same:

A few brave people decided they were tired of waiting.

Tired of waiting for outside investors.

Tired of waiting for perfect timing.

Tired of waiting for permission.

So they started. Small.

They hosted casual meetups in coffee shops.

They launched scrappy pilots on shoestring budgets.

They walked across institutional lines and asked new questions.

They listened, I mean really listened, to what local founders needed.

They rallied unlikely allies: school leaders, neighborhood pastors, librarians, barbers, and bank tellers.

They built things not just for the community, but with it.

And slowly, what once seemed improbable began to feel possible. Then practical. Then inevitable.

Not because the city had every advantage.
Not because they secured a million-dollar grant.

Not because a celebrity endorsed them or a tech giant moved in.

But because someone believed.

Believed that innovation could come from within.

Believed that talent already lived there.

Believed that small wins could lead to big change if they kept showing up.

That someone might be you.

You don't need a title. You don't need a perfect plan. You need the courage to care, the patience to build, and the vision to see your city not for what it has been, but for what it could be.

Because ecosystems don't begin with infrastructure.

They begin with belief.

And belief? That's something every city can afford.

All it needs is someone to plant the first seed.

The Warning Signs Are Real. But So Are the Opportunities

I can tell you from experience that this work is hard. Building a startup ecosystem in a small city is not for the faint of heart. It will stretch you, test you, and at times, it will wear you down.

You will face resistance.

There will be people who question your vision, who ask why this matters, who cling tightly to the way things have always been. You may hear, "We tried that before," or "That won't work here," or my personal favorite, "Why would we want chickens downtown," more times than you can count. And, yes, I really did get asked that last one.

There will be power struggles.

Competing agendas, turf wars, egos, and institutional inertia—all of it will show up when you least need it. Even among well-meaning partners, collaboration can get messy.

Funding will be tight.

You'll write grants late at night. Stretch dollars that shouldn't stretch. You'll wonder if anyone else sees the value in this work the way you do.

And yes, momentum will come and go.

There will be seasons of incredible progress and seasons where nothing seems to move. Events will fall flat. Initiatives will stall. People will leave. Doubt will creep in.

But here's the part too many cities miss:

The biggest risk isn't failure.

It's inaction.

It's watching the same barriers go unchallenged.

It's letting outdated narratives define your future.

It's waiting for someone else to bring the solution.

When we choose to do nothing, we don't just pause progress. We reinforce the belief that nothing better is possible. And that belief, left unchallenged, becomes the real threat to a community's future.

So yes, the warning signs are real. But so are the opportunities—especially for those bold enough to lean in anyway.

You don't need permission to start.

You don't need to have all the answers.

What you really need, though, are:

- Partners who are just as dedicated as you are—even if they aren't fluent in your language just yet;

- Perseverance during the slow times when you can't see any improvement yet the seeds are taking root;

- Plan that is bold but also grounded and adaptable. One that doesn't just include a list of things to do but also a clear vision for your people and your place.

Because in the end, ecosystems don't rise because everything went smoothly. They rise because someone refused to let their city be defined by limitation.

That someone might be you.

Ecosystem Building Is Never "Done"

If you've made it this far, you might be wondering: When does the work start to feel complete? When do we finally "arrive" as an ecosystem?

The honest answer?

You don't.

Because ecosystem building is never truly finished. It's not a five-year plan with a neat bow at the end. It's not a simple checklist that you complete and move on from. It's a living, breathing process that requires constant attention, adjustment, and care.

Even the most advanced ecosystems, the ones that get featured in national publications or cited in economic development playbooks, are still evolving. Still learning. Still facing new challenges they didn't see coming.

This is an important part of ecosystem building because there will always be:

- New founders stepping up with fresh ideas, fresh energy, and new needs that your ecosystem must be ready to support.

- New industries emerging, shaped by shifting technologies, market demands, and community priorities.

- New equity gaps to address, because no system is immune to exclusion, and closing those gaps takes more than good intentions.

- New policies and public agendas to shape that coincide with civic leadership changes, funding model shifts, and new opportunities.

- New stories to tell that reflect the next generation of builders so that they see themselves in the narrative of what's possible.

So think of this work not as a sprint. Not even as a marathon.

But as a relay.

Your job isn't to run forever.

Your job is to run well and to build with care, to lead with integrity, and to learn what works and what doesn't.

And then? Pass the baton.

Pass it with documentation. Pass it with mentorship. Pass it by making sure your systems aren't dependent on a single person or a single moment. Pass it in a way that ensures the next generation is better equipped than the last.

Because that's how true progress works.

It's not about who crosses the finish line.

It's about building a track that others can run farther on.

And if you've done that—if you've built something that lasts beyond you—then you haven't just supported startups.

You've started a legacy.

This Is Your Moment

Let me leave you with this simple thought. Small cities are no longer waiting in the wings. They are not simply watching from the sidelines as big metros capture the headlines and hoard all the capital. Quietly but steadily, they're becoming the places where new possibilities take root. Where people can take chances and ideas aren't drowned out by noise. They are the spots where being close to someone may turn them into a partner, and inspiring a neighbor can turn them into a startup ecosystem champion.

In these cities, affordability meets ambition. And their size is their competitive advantage.

Not every founder has to raise a seed round to survive. And not every program needs a six-figure sponsor to be meaningful.

In small cities, what you build can matter right away. And when people see that their efforts have an immediate impact, momentum becomes contagious.

In these cities, relationships move faster than red tape.

The mayor lives down the street.

The college dean shows up to the coworking mixer.

The banker sponsoring your pitch night also coached your kid's Little League team.

This kind of proximity is power.

And in a world that often values quantity over substance, small cities offer something that can't be manufactured. They offer authenticity, resilience, and community.

These are not obstacles to innovation.

They are its foundation.

So whether you're a founder with an idea that won't let you sleep…

A funder looking to invest in people over prestige…

A public servant ready to unlock policy and potential…

An educator nurturing the next generation of builders…

Or a neighbor who simply believes your city deserves more.

This is your moment.

You don't need to wait for a national spotlight, a celebrity endorsement, or a massive grant to begin.

You don't need to follow someone else's playbook or ask permission to care.

You can shape the future of your city.

You can build something real, something lasting, and something that outlives any headline or trend.

You are the ecosystem.

You are the culture, the momentum, and the connective tissue.

So step forward. Start small. Dream bigger.

Because innovation doesn't live in a zip code.

It lives in people willing to build.

INDEX